What God Had Emptied

How I Found Hope
in My Children's Diagnoses

Kathryn Anne Casey

En Route Books and Media, LLC
Saint Louis, MO

En Route Books and Media, LLC

5705 Rhodes Avenue

St. Louis, MO 63109

Contact us at contactus@enroutebooksandmedia.com

Cover credit: Kathryn Anne Casey with "The Holy Family" by Henry Ossawa Tanner (1910) on Wikiart at https://www.wikiart.org/en/henry-ossawa-tanner/the-holy-family-1910

ISBN-13: 978-1-956715-61-3

Library of Congress Control Number: 2022941221

Dedicated to my husband, Kyle.

We faced these trials of life from far apart and near each other. We have laughed, cried, waited and worried together, always together, no matter how far apart we were. I could not have shared this story without you. I could not have faced this story without you. I love you.

Acknowledgments

I would like to express my gratitude to all those who helped bring this story to publication. First and foremost, my husband, Kyle, and my parents, Thomas and Patricia McGuire, who kept the fires burning on the home front, maintaining as much stability as possible for our children while Peter and I stayed at UCSF. To my children, who may not remember these events after so many years have passed, but whose joy and unwavering trust inspired us to keep doing the best we could no matter how difficult things got, especially Miriam, who as the oldest child has had to jump more than once in a crisis and does it beautifully.

To the many doctors and departments of UCSF who helped Peter thrive, the GI Department, the Transitional Care Unit doctors and nurses, Dr. Sue Rhee, Dr. Phil Rosenthal, Dr. Vivek Chenoy, and especially, Dr. Amanda Posner, whose love and dedication to my son and our family changed our lives. To the UCSF FLIGHT Team, who helped me become the medical mother I am today, especially Dr. Duncan Henry and Amy Chang. To the rest of our support team from UCSF, Summer Segal, Rebecca Gates, Peg Langham, and the nurse whose words and support were a regular refuge for me, Sharon.

To the friends and spiritual supporters during these two years: my aunt Pam Pantell, and friends, Camille Iorns, Lauren Miller, and Tori Zeek whose regular correspondence while we were in San Francisco were a lifeline. My Aunt Corrine, who walked those first steps with me into our hospital life. Fr. Bill McDonald, whose words were a light in a time of great darkness. And my dear friend Erin Fernandez, who not only emailed regularly but came to stay with our family for the days after Celeste's birth, making it possible for Kyle and me to grieve together and grow back together after so much time apart.

And lastly, to Dr. Sebastian Mahfood, OP, and the team at En Route Books and Media who dived in ready to share this story with the world as a celebration of our children's lives, no matter how brief they may be.

Table of Contents

Part III: The Sorrowful Mysteries

Part IV: The Glorious Mysteries

Introduction

In memoirs, we seek to share the moments of a single story. This account, enclosed in a two-year period, holds more moments than can be adequately expressed by a single narrative. It is but one perspective of the events that took place. It tells the tale of two years, two positive pregnancy tests, two prenatal diagnoses, and two different outcomes.

However unique our experiences, as Christians, we can unite our journey to Christ and know that all we experience, he has experienced. The Blessed Virgin Mary has been there. We learn this particularly through meditation of the Rosary. As I began to weave together the individual moments of these two years, I saw the pattern of the fabric align with the narrative arc of the Rosary which directs our consideration of Mary's life with Christ.

The Rosary, a traditional prayer of the Catholic Church, began as a way of praying the Psalms for those who could not read. An apparition of the Virgin Mary to St. Dominic in 1217 gave it the structure and focus we know today: one Our Father, ten Hail Marys, one Glory Be, each decade focused on a mystery of Christ's life from conception to his glory in Heaven. Like the events of this story, these mysteries do not refer to matters to be solved, but instead supernatural truths whose innermost nature lies beyond what we can know by logic or reason.

The rhythm of the rosary alternates from the Lord's Prayer, begging God's divine assistance, His presence, and His Fatherly care, to the fiat of Mary in the Hail Mary, entrusting the soul to the will of God. The decade of Hail Marys ends with recognizing God's everlasting glory in the Glory Be.

So through this prayer, we discover not only the pattern of our lives, seen in Christ's life, but we discover the answers as well when we come face to face with the challenge to trust in the Lord following a unique and, perhaps, terrifying call, and the promise of his reward. I was a young woman, a happily married mother of three, born into a Catholic family, raised in a Catholic family and formed by daily mass and a typical youth group in a small farming community in California. As a zealous youth, I took my example from St. Thérèse of Lisieux, when offered all by God, I said, "I choose everything."

Nearing the end of a year of missionary work with the National Evangelization Team, I knelt. I knelt in the wood-paneled chapel of the Missionaries of the Holy Spirit below the hill of Mount Angel, Oregon, where the sight of the Eucharist centered on the heart of a gold Cross filled my soul with joy. The gentle words, "do you accept this?" passed through my mind. Overcome with awe, I answered yes with all my heart.

It would be years before I set out on the journey that would ask me to stand by that decision. I married at 24, birthed my first child at 25, and alternated between working for a local non-profit and staying home with the home-schooling bunch while my husband built his business.

This story tells of fear, uncertainty, and grief, but also shares a mother's love and effort to accept her child's presence in her womb and in the hospital bed. It tells of the growth possible in challenging circumstances and of the remarkable discovery that when we offer our hearts without reservation to the One who is all-faithful and all-good, He will ask us to walk the way he walked, the mysterious journey through the cross and the hope of resurrection.

Part I

The Joyful Mysteries

Chapter 1

The Annunciation

But she was greatly troubled at what was said and pondered what sort of greeting this might be.... Mary said to the angel, "How can this be...?" (Luke 1:29, 34)

The pregnancy test lay by the bathroom sink as I sat on the corner of the bed beside my husband, reclined against the watercolor print pillows. White, cotton-percale sheets and a faded turquoise coverlet dressed the bed, under an ikebana print duvet folded in thirds every morning at its foot.

My smile was at one-third power. Interiorly moved but outwardly calm, I revealed the news. He was surprised...though not entirely. To encourage him, I said, "I'm happy about this."

"You are?" He made an effort to be happy, too. With three other offspring under age five asleep two doors down the hallway, his desire for sleep was stronger than his desire for children at that moment.

The transition to three children was the hardest so far. As with past experiences, once I mastered it, I was ready to tackle the next new thing. Conscious of my happiness, he opened his heart to be happy, too.

"Happy Mother's Day," he sighed.

The watching and waiting and wondering began. Weeks seven to nine were the most fearful time for me. The first miscarriage ended my first pregnancy at seven weeks; the second miscarriage ended my third pregnancy at nine weeks. Now, at week eight, overwhelmed by anxiety, I was done with this waiting and wondering. I plodded into the Modesto Pregnancy Center for a free sonogram, thinking, *I have to know*. Another month of waiting for my insurance to cover this was too much to ask of my anxiety.

The little bean on the screen wiggled. He was there, alive. It was too early for a heartbeat, but the movement was enough for me to breathe again.

Did I overreact? Should I not have worried?

If I did miscarry, I would have faced it. We could have gotten through it. The words challenged me like a stranger in a mirror.

With such reassurance, I delayed my appointment with the doctor. At 18 weeks, I listened to the heartbeat, took a deep breath and braced myself to endure another routine pregnancy. We scheduled the 20-week ultrasound.

That summer, I switched from early intervention sessions with at-risk high school students to the marketing department at the Center for Human Services. My work moved from the frigid, beige high school office to the brand new, industrial chic agency building. Wardrobe options shrank as my size grew. Some identified the growing belly. Interactions with coworkers and strangers required witty repartee to counterbalance their contemplation of my family size.

Family life made working eight-hour days untenable. I explored what step to take next. The work I did at the agency could be freelanced. Adults and teenagers could benefit from the coping and life skills I taught in schools. Without the contract hours to fill working for the agency, I could leave when the client work was done. The response of my graduate professor, Dr. Nordling, to my inquiry read that this project sounded like life coaching, a more marketable term than what I had in mind. Within a few weeks, I completed an online certification program and became a life coach.

As summer ended, I turned in my letter of resignation. Our HR director, Dawn Tacker understood. From across the desk she said, "It's a lot to manage with four at home."

Everyone congratulated me on my next child, a career as a life coach and small business owner.

If I started the business now, I could give myself maternity leave in January when the baby came. Once I adjusted to life with four children, I could pick up where I left off. The investment was time-consuming, stressful and a little expensive. Getting started required the most energy. Yet, there was more energy now than there would be the first year after delivery. Pregnancy was predictable. All three had been the same.

By October, I rented the office, painted and hung art prints and my diplomas on the wall. The website was under construction; the dreams were big. As a way to advertise my expertise and services without cost to me, I went about writing a weekly column in the *Hughson Chronicle*, a local print-only newspaper part of Midvalley Publications promoting "The Power of the Positive Press."

With every plan in place, all I had to do was follow the steps. Whether things went as planned or varied mattered not. Watching plans unfold makes life interesting.

The nurse guided my husband, four-year-old daughter and me into the dimmed, ultrasound room, with robin's egg walls, for my 20-week scan. At four-years-old, Miriam was old enough to understand, pay attention to the screen and enjoy hearing the announcement of the baby's sex.

My neck ached from trying to see the screen. The baby flexed on the screen just beyond my view. This middle-aged woman with short blonde hair and obnoxiously loud scrubs held off turning the screen towards me until she had all the measurements. With warm gel on my stomach, I pretended to be patient. To pass the time, I interjected here and there, fishing once, "I just want to know he's okay."

The woman intoned, "I've almost never seen anything that can't be fixed." Her words passed by me as her hands dragged the wand along my stomach.

The excitement waned, and I grew bored. The technician rotated the screen and declared, "It's a boy!"

Oh, boy, another boy. We were in the throes of James' two-year-old wildness. We seemed to draw a collective breath of acceptance together. The ultrasound was over. She printed the pictures, wiped the gel with a towel and left the room. We returned to the latte and chocolate-colored exam room.

The midwife returned to talk with us. Carolyn used a forearm crutch on one arm to balance her, as an effect of a childhood case of polio. Her chestnut hair was thrown back in a ponytail. The years of wisdom and experience wore on her face. She had journeyed with me already through two joyful pregnancies. She came in quietly, looking at me steadily, not a bit routine. Something was different. "Is everything okay?" I asked.

The words came through strain and fog. My feet dangled awkwardly from the exam table. Carolyn spelled out facts about cleft lips and palates, when the roof the mouth and upper lip fail to close completely during development, and surgeries. She added, if you had to choose one defect, she would choose this because it can be fixed.

The baby can live a normal life.

There would be surgery.

With a cleft palate, there will not be nursing.

There will not be nursing.

Carolyn kept talking. As the words penetrated my understanding, the tears welled up. There will not be nursing.

"Can you take Miriam out?" I whispered to Kyle in order to hide my tears from her. He ushered her out. Kyle left, and I stayed.

Carolyn earned my trust when she eased my fears at my first prenatal appointment with Regina following a miscarriage. Carolyn expounded, and I nodded my head, trying to grasp the information. The storm of thoughts pulled me down. Leaning forward, I took it in and embraced it.

We reviewed the plan. There would be a referral, then a call for another ultrasound. Drying my eyes, I left the room, walked down the hallway and found Kyle and Miriam sitting in the waiting room beyond the double doors. We left.

"I guess we will name him Peter Solanus," I proposed to Kyle. The name was one we considered before the birth of James, our second born, whose name was chosen to honor family and the faith.

"Yeah, that sounds right," Kyle agreed. The name was a solace in the situation.

A great fog settled on our home. Talking and thinking became tiresome. The children required responses. All morning in a stupor, I alternated between a depressed silence and sobbing. To my oldest daughter, I only said we had to find a new doctor for the baby. It was fearful even to write because I thought if I started to cry I might not be able to stop again until it was time to sleep.

When I woke, my head cleared.

It would be okay. That was clear the moment Carolyn diagnosed him. We would find the doctor we needed. It would be okay. Whatever the downfalls of the medical profession, they do a lot, even for those who cannot pay. But because we could not pay, I felt powerless. Where could I turn?

The bigness of the problem made me cry. I could not see through it or around it or above it. So I cried.

It was the shock. We found out yesterday. Tomorrow would be better. *Perhaps, I should wait until the shock subsides before trying to do anything.*

Writing or talking without crying seemed impossible. I wanted to stare into space on my bed, my mind was numb.

Why was I reacting this way? It must be the shock. In my head, I knew it would be okay. Yet I was powerless and small. The thing loomed large in front of me, too big to see around or beyond.

I had to carry on. It was time to get up.

Sugey arrived to pick an almond branch from my parents' orchard for a homeschool project. We knew each other through the years, Catholic acquaintances thrown together through parish and diocesan events. We visited these days for me to learn from her parenting. Eagerly I unloaded my heart with this friend. We ambled into the orchard and paused at the beginning of the rows, where older trees grew alongside "The Woods," an old horse corral where I played as a girl. The trees' verdant leaves faded to sage, burdened with almonds ready to harvest. Once shaken by harvesters, the leaves would seem weak and dead.

In tears, I poured out the news: the cleft, no nursing, the surgery. Everything was uncertain as we waited for confirmation through another ultrasound. Could be a cleft palate.

Might not be a cleft palate. Cleft palate meant no nursing. No cleft palate meant there is a chance of nursing. The words threatened my mind, forcing it to stand precariously between despair and hope.

She had been there, too. Not with a cleft, but out of her large family, many experiences were borne. Her first child could not nurse. For another child, the doctor predicted birth defects and recommended abortion. She refused. Another had emergency surgery after she found a diaper full of blood. "It is the worst feeling in the world to hand your child off for surgery," she empathized.

Sugey got through it. I would, too. After talking, my thoughts quieted down again.

We walked back around beside The Woods, between the green and red tractors, across the gravel driveway, to the porch where my family was. We stood in the driveway a while longer talking about less important things. She climbed into her white Honda Odyssey and drove one mile to her home to show her boys the almond branch.

Chapter 2

The Visitation

And how does this happen to me, that the mother of my Lord should come to me? For at the moment the sound of your greeting reached my ears, the infant in my womb leaped for joy. (Luke 1:43-44)

The woman on the end of the telephone informed me we would see Dr. Slocum. It was not often I took up the rosary in those days. Before marriage I prayed daily but I never managed to capture the routine once children came along. Now I prayed to prepare my heart. Fingering pine beads from Assisi, I peered into the mysteries through a lens of the unknown before us, the unknown we would discover that day.

At the first Our Father, the Annunciation, I saw our Lady with great faith accepting her child, opening herself up to the vulnerability of motherhood.

With the second Our Father begins the Visitation of Mary to Elizabeth. Here Mary still offers out the good inside her. Even with the warnings she received, she sought to serve others, suffering in the process. It was long and difficult to travel.

During the third Our Father, the Nativity, there is a strangeness here. One hears the whispers of glory and greatness. Mary wondered at the events surrounding her child's birth. How she must have suffered, unable to prepare a proper place for her son, unable to find a place to rest until just before his birth, without the safety of family and home.

Through the fourth Our Father, the prophets plant the foreshadowing of future suffering in the Presentation in the Temple. With a flourish, Simeon prophesied her suffering. Even in joyful things, a warning of what is to come passes between them. God prepares her heart by teaching her to embrace, with courage, wherever this path of motherhood takes her.

Then in the fifth Our Father, the Finding in the Temple, Christ sets his mother's *via dolorosa* in motion. The child is missing. The terror she must have felt! When she found him, he is already about his father's work. He is not her possession. Without a fight, she let him go. "Stop holding on to me," Christ told Mary Magdalene after the Resurrection (John 20:17). The frantic search for him foreshadows the terrible loss she will experience when he reaches maturity.

The rosary ends. The nurse calls my name. She opens the door. Our hands together, Kyle and I pass through the door to the hallway, another door and into Dr. Slocum's office.

We looked at Slocum and listened through stacks of paper piled high on his executive-size desk and listened as he breathed heavily. His white shirt, white hair and white goatee painted the portrait of Colonel Sanders. While he examined the sonogram pictures, my eyes crawled up his wall of books.

Setting the papers down decisively he said, "Looks just like a cleft lip...I can't say definitively, but I would say I am nearly 100% sure he does not have a cleft palate."

It could have been much worse. No cleft palate...nearly 100%, he said. Thank God! Nursing! I emailed family and friends. The University of California, San Francisco or Stanford would contact us next.

But, Slocum was wrong.

The drive to UCSF lit up the sciatic pain in my backside. After three hours of ultrasounds reclining on my pregnant back, the new doctor began her review, "So yes... as the other doctor wrote, bilateral cleft lip and palate—"

"What!" With a pause to stay calm, "We thought it was only a cleft lip."

No. It is both. The rest of what she said blurred together. She walked us back to the waiting room.

In the 8x10-foot private waiting room of the Fetal Treatment Center, the news sank in. We pretended to be interested in large framed kid-style art mounted on the walls. At least Baby's heart was good.

"Put that in your backpack," the late Sr. Lucero would have said to me. I visited her twice a week throughout high school and on vacations during college. We stood outside the adoration chapel of the Sisters of the Cross, neglecting our prayer, but growing in every other way. Put that in your backpack, she once told me at the end of a letter full of advice. I should store this news too for later. Can we leave the rest behind?

The facts poured in. Nurse Practitioner Peg Langham poured them in for us:

- Within a couple weeks of his birth, we will go to UCSF again.
- At 3-4 months of age, they will operate to close the cleft lip.
- At 10-12 months of age, they will operate to fix the cleft palate.

- With both surgeries, he will be expected to stay overnight at UCSF. As his parents, we are able to stay with him in the room on those nights.

Peg introduced us to the specialty cleft bottle; the brands Pigeon, Dr. Brown's and Haberman; and how they work without requiring suction. The hole in the roof of the infant's mouth prevents him from forming a seal through which to suck. The bottles are designed for the child to push down with his gums in order to release the milk.

All this information was in black and white. The way she detailed it sounded routine. It did not feel routine.

All I could do was quip, "So what you're saying is...our baby doesn't suck."

The weeks passed. Four weeks before my due date, for the first time since that 20-week sonogram rocked my world, I felt sublimely happy to have a baby.

It started with a bizarre, pregnancy-affected dream. While Kyle slept, I dreamt I awoke to the baby's moving and pushing on the walls around him. Instead of the usual bump indicating a hand or a foot pressing against the sides of my uterus, baby's entire arm from fingertip to elbow was visible through my skin. This seemed normal. In the dream, I roused my husband to show him. Moving the turquoise blanket away, there he was, all of him, lying happily on the white sheets. Peter was born.

How did that happen? Inside my dream, I woke up wondering, *Did he come out of my side like that freakish arm? Was this the moment from Alien?* The dream revealed I delivered him the normal way, only I was asleep.

Then, I held him.

I held my son in my arms.

Some dreams powerfully capture your imagination for days following, such that you cannot look at certain people without recalling the emotion of the dream. Just so, this dream captured my heart.

Surgery, lips, NAM appliances that seem to tape the lips together leading up to surgery, pumping, special bottles, holes in the roof of his mouth ceased to matter. Nothing mattered. My son would be born.

Tears of joy fought for air on the way to my OB check-up. When Carolyn walked in and began the discussion, I told her of my joy. After walking with me through the shock, depression and fear that came with wrapping my mind around the future, she felt my joy and hugged me.

Nothing mattered now. All that mattered was to hold him in my arms.

Chapter 3

The Nativity

And Mary kept all these things, reflecting on them in her heart. (Luke 2:19)

Dear Peter,

On Mother's Day, we learned you existed. It was happy news; it really was, even with having our three wild ones. You were wanted.

I was so frightened I would lose you. For reassurance, I asked for a sonogram at the pregnancy center. And there you were, a little nugget, bouncing around the screen. I loved you.

Our next sonogram, you were 20 weeks along. That is when they told us you would have a cleft lip and possibly a cleft palate. I was scared to lose you, scared to lose breast-feeding, bonding, our connection. Most of all, I was scared to lose you.

At the next sonogram, the doctor said you did not have a cleft palate. What joy we felt. This meant you could breast-feed. It felt like everything would be okay if I could breast-feed you, if I could nourish you, bond with you and take care of you.

The next sonogram was in San Francisco, the place where we would later spend a great deal of time. We faced the grief all over again. Part way through the in-depth sono-gram, looking into your eyes, I saw you; and I loved you.

We waited; I grieved. We bought bottles and anticipated the shock of meeting you with pictures of babies with cleft lips. Some babies with clefts stop breathing at night. We

19

bought a monitor that could detect if the baby stopped moving. I didn't want to lose you. Whatever it takes, we would protect you.

I grieved more. What would we have if I could not breastfeed you? We questioned God, why was this happening, why should you suffer? I ached for you.

Then, something happened. I dreamt of a mysterious birth and you lying beside me. It strengthened me. Whatever would happen, we would face it. We could face it.

You were born. The nurse said it was the best delivery she had ever seen, so calm, so peaceful. It did not take long. You were smaller than expected. At the sonogram you measured big. Maybe it is all connected.

On my chest, you found your way to the breast. Some colostrum dribbled out of your wide-open, cleft-lipped mouth. You were beautiful. Your face was smooth, just as I had seen on the sonogram when I looked into your eyes on that fuzzy screen. I recognized you; I knew you.

It did not matter that your face looked flat, that the columella was missing, that strip of skin running from the tip of the nose to the upper lip, separating the nostrils. At first glance, we could not see a nose. All I saw were your eyes.

They rolled you away in your bassinet to the Newborn Intensive Care Unit to observe your breathing and eating. The pediatrician warned us that you might need a feeding tube. The nurse won my affection by taking me to say goodnight to you before taking me to my room. It was good to see where you would rest. Visualizing you kept me connected to you.

You were fine. You fed well from the bottle, and always have. Everyone said so. The sight of you the next morning overwhelmed me, and I began to cry. Your cleft seemed so big. The petite, Chinese NICU nurse drew the curtain around us and suggested skin-to-skin contact. Holding you thus, my heart returned to me. You were mine, and I loved you.

When the nurse brought you to my room, I pumped and gave you the bottle. At that time, I did not realize how over time the bottle would be our bond, or that you would always want to be held. You would co-sleep because we could not put you down. How I loved to sleep beside you, hear you breathe and gurgle noisily through that cleft, knowing you were alive. I gazed at your face, smiling at your success with the bottle.

At your first appointment at UCSF, we met the plastic surgeon, Dr. William Hoffman, as he rushed in excusing his tardiness by referencing "mayhem in the OR." He put his gloved finger in your mouth and said, "I just want to see if I can feel any brain coming through…I can't." Hoffman says it how it is.

It was hard: hard to feed you, hard to get you to gain weight. During a night of tears when you threw up, again and again, God said to me in a vision, "I will take him to the throne room. He is my son. I love him."

At your baptism, we waited in the oak pews of the chapel where I first loved God and wanted to give my life to him. This was the throne room. Fr. Raju repeated the words the Father spoke as Christ came out of the water, "This is my beloved Son."

He said you are God's son.

He said God loved you.

A month has passed since we came to this hospital. More than anything, I miss sleeping with you in my arms.

You did not gain weight. We tried everything with the bottle. You kept spitting up. Then the stomach flu visited all of us. First, the children caught it, then me, then you. You vomited more and began to get diarrhea. It was terrifying. Twice, we visited the Emergency Department...twice. The second time was in the middle of the night. "He's below his birth weight," I told them.

Why would they not admit you? Why would they not keep you safe?

In conversation with Peg every day, we agreed that if you looked worse on the day of your Ophthalmology appointment at UCSF, she would walk us over to the ED at Benioff Children's Hospital, part of UCSF, the opposite end of the clinic building.

We drove. She saw. You were admitted.

Walking into the Pediatric Intensive Care Unit (PICU), I fell apart. It was like the movies with all that equipment and a strange little bassinet under a heat lamp. The equipment formed a wall. The couch was behind the wall by the window. There we parked and whispered, staring at the back of the crib and through glass sliding doors. When you heard my voice, you cried. Mostly, you slept. There was nothing I could do. I felt useless, helpless and in a trance.

All you did was sleep. You hardly moved. Your sodium was dangerously low.

It was a nightmare to see you on all those monitors. I was scared to lose you. Barely thinking...or breathing, I thought we would lose you.

††††

WELCOME TO HOLLAND

By Emily Perl Kingsley.

I am often asked to describe the experience of raising a child with a disability - to try to help people who have not shared that unique experience to understand it, to imagine how it would feel. It's like this......

When you're going to have a baby, it's like planning a fabulous vacation trip - to Italy. You buy a bunch of guide books and make your wonderful plans. The Coliseum. The Michelangelo David. The gondolas in Venice. You may learn some handy phrases in Italian. It's all very exciting.

After months of eager anticipation, the day finally arrives. You pack your bags and off you go. Several hours later, the plane lands. The stewardess comes in and says, "Welcome to Holland."

"Holland?!?" you say. "What do you mean Holland?? I signed up for Italy! I'm supposed to be in Italy. All my life I've dreamed of going to Italy."

But there's been a change in the flight plan. They've landed in Holland and there you must stay.

The important thing is that they haven't taken you to a horrible, disgusting, filthy place, full of pestilence, famine and disease. It's just a different place.

So you must go out and buy new guide books. And you must learn a whole new language. And you will meet a whole new group of people you would never have met.

It's just a different place. It's slower-paced than Italy, less flashy than Italy. But after you've been there for a while and you catch your breath, you look around.... and you begin to notice that Holland has windmills....and Holland has tulips. Holland even has Rembrandts.

But everyone you know is busy coming and going from Italy... and they're all bragging about what a wonderful time they had there. And for the rest of your life, you will say "Yes, that's where I was supposed to go. That's what I had planned."

And the pain of that will never, ever, ever, ever go away... because the loss of that dream is a very very significant loss.

But... if you spend your life mourning the fact that you didn't get to Italy, you may never be free to enjoy the very special, the very lovely things ... about Holland.[1]

---

[1] Emily Perl Kingsley. Used with permission.

Chapter 4

The Flight to Egypt

When they had departed, behold, the angel of the Lord appeared to Joseph in a dream and said, "Rise, take the child and his mother, flee to Egypt, and stay there until I tell you. (Matthew 2:13)

The first four days passed. No one could say when we would leave. Kyle's work provided no paid leave or vacation time.

Kyle left and I stayed.

Peg visited every day. When Peter's electrolytes stabilized, we transitioned from the PICU to the "floor," the Medical/Surgical General Unit.

There was a private bathroom.

The room offered privacy enough to pump, but little help with Peter. My modesty longed for privacy. The stronger Peter grew, the more help I needed. He cried, begging to be held. Two feet from him, hooked up to a rented Medela, I could not comfort him.

A Patient Care Assistant named Dustin, young, high-voiced and slight-statured, did not overwhelm me. He helped cheerfully and often to fill in the gaps left by Cally, Peter's Australian and intimidating nurse with a penchant for medical terminology. When I asked for help, her comments on how little time she had burdened me. When she said we should think about putting in a g-tube, it troubled me. A gastronomy tube is surgically inserted into the stomach so food can be delivered directly, without using the mouth.

Our room was situated at the end of the unit hallway. A large window took parents on mental vacations when they peered out into the San Francisco Bay and remarked on the vast cruise ship docked there. Every day, I checked to see if it was still in the harbor.

At morning rounds, the team of doctors met together discussing Peter. In this setting, they introduced Gastroenterology (GI) for the first time. Michelle Long, the attending doctor whose voice resounded emphatically with each statement, hoped we could go home that day. My heart flew at the thought. Then Dr. Yvette Wild, attending GI doctor, disagreed. She hated to say it, but GI's opinion carried more weight.

I stayed on my feet for the news. Only later did I sit in that lime green hospital recliner, attached to the pump, gripping Pooja's hand, sobbing uncontrollably. To this caring third-year resident doctor in medical school, I managed the words out between sobs: "I haven't seen my children in a week." With her sure and soothing voice, she made me feel there was a way forward.

That was a night of tears, drowning in the emotion and stress of a week alone with my baby in the hospital. The next day, Eunice, a social worker, came to talk with me. "You need to get out," she exhorted. "You should take a walk."

Her words pushed me out the door. After she left, when the emotion welled up again, I was no longer mourning.

I was fed up.

Leaning into her urging from the hour before, I got out.

I went for a walk.

In a haze, I bought Haribo gold bears and a body pouf at the tiny Walgreens across the street from the clinic building. It was a normal thing to buy things, unlike the week I had been living.

Walking sounds tame. It is not.

In a fury, I walked, lengthening my stride. As I walked and continued walking, the rhythm of the steps overcame my thoughts. The pace of my breathing out-paced the emotion surging in my heart. I kept on walking until my eyes shifted focus from inward to outward. Buildings came into focus. The sky came into focus. I felt the breeze again. The drowning stopped and the scene around me came into color. I felt curious.

When this happened, I recognized my location. It was 3rd Street. Maybe this was where Kyle walked when he went to Safeway those first few days. It was not very scenic. The ports looked abandoned between a sea of concrete and the San Francisco Bay. Invigorated by the clear skies, clean air and enveloping sunshine, I followed the sign to the nostalgia-inducing AT&T Park.

I walked on. Approaching the park, a snack shack sold beer. The steel members of Lefty O'Doul Bridge stretched across a stench of water. Businesspeople walked and homeless people milled about. Outside the Dugout Store, a sign advertised ballpark tours. It would be wonderful to see the inside. Not since third grade have I cared about baseball. Stepping inside, I inquired of the clerk the cost of tours: "$22."

Yikes. "Make-a-buck. Make-a-buck. Don't care what [baseball] stands for, just make-a-buck, make-a-buck." I walked on.

Turning the curved corner around the stadium, across the street stood Momo's. Its black and tan striped awnings and serif typeface beckoned me. I was hungry and sick of hospital food. The food was palatable but dry, and the repetition drove me mad. Momo's drew me. The host handed me a menu. Dismissing the high prices, a Freudian Id power propelled the moment forward. Impulsively, I asked, "How is your French Dip?"

"Excellent," he responded.

"Can I get it boxed up?" He directed me to order from the bar. Self-consciously, I chose a seat. "Can I get you something to drink while you wait?"

Blushing, I stumbled, "oh, no" like a sheltered house-wife.

The bartender offered water. Maybe he meant that from the start.

I ordered, drank my water and paid for my $18 French Dip sandwich. It felt wonderful to spend a lavish amount of money on something. The smell tantalized.

Time to return. One hour had passed since I left.

In the presence of the day's resident, Jen, and a nurse practitioner I ate my French Dip. *This was good,* I thought, *good to walk, good to feel free, good to spend.* Goodness was a feeling I had not felt in a while.

The next day when I stepped outside that good feeling returned. Surveying my surroundings, I wondered, *Where should I go now? Adventure is out there. AT&T Park yesterday. The Design Center today?* To walk and eat at the same time appeared casual and cool. Whole Foods was down Mariposa Street. When we examined Google maps, Jen described this route was safe. I prepared to go.

The walk began. There was no fog that day, only curiosity. My attention heightened as I followed the sidewalk under the freeway, scanning for suspicious characters. Graffiti decorated each pillar alongside the train tracks. The road led uphill. My legs sensed it. It was good to use them again.

To the left stood a hardware store. To the right: a dog grooming shop. Buildings triggered thoughts of my own home, questioning if charcoal window casings would complement cream siding or if it would be too dramatic. Painted lady houses inspired awe. Modern architecture punctuated the iconic Victorian homes one expects in San Francisco. History and architecture enchanted me. The colors were visionary.

Signs at Whole Foods reminded me tomorrow was St. Patrick's Day. I wanted to buy beer. I wanted to buy wine. I wanted to buy the whole store. Ten minutes passed as I weighed my options in the candy aisle, calculating the price per ounce because we always joked about Whole Foods being more aptly called "Whole Paycheck."

Newman's Own sour licorice ropes in cherry won the debate, as did hairspray. A new product might help this mess. Sun blasted through the exit as I ventured back out to the street. Signs pointed to the Design Center.

A tile store distracted me first. On the entryway wall to the left, I discovered the perfect marble herringbone mosaic for our foyer. A black ash with patina cut into a 12x24 inch piece was meant for our fireplace. The clerk copied the pricing information. In our small talk, I shared how I love planning a design concept. "Oh, you should be a planner," she fanned my flattery. The city is completely changing, she informed me.

In taking the samples, I left some heaviness behind. It stayed that way as I reentered the hospital. There was not enough time to reach the Design Center that day. Rebecca, Peter's social worker who dressed in business causal and flat, always with a black leather shoulder bag, indulged my design talk over the tile samples. The patients at UCSF all get a social worker. They get an attending doctor in charge, a resident to visit you daily, a nurse that changes every 12 hours, a

Patient Care Assistant, a Child Life Specialist and a social worker. The lucky ones have inpatient specialists added, in our case a GI attending doctor and GI fellow just out of school studying the specialty. All of these people checked on me now that I had cried my eyes out in their presence. But Rebecca did not ask about my tears; she asked about the walks. These tile samples and brochures filled my mind with plans for my Hughson home.

Chapter 5

The Presentation in the Temple

Simeon blessed them and said to Mary his mother, "Behold, this child is destined for the fall and rise of many in Israel, and to be a sign that will be contradicted (and you yourself a sword will pierce) so that the thoughts of many hearts may be revealed." (Luke 2:32-33)

The eleven days passed. A narrow buttercup-yellow tube accompanied us home, inserted down my son's throat until it reached his stomach. If it is taped to his cheek and goes in his mouth and down the throat, GI explained, it is called an OG tube. O is for Oral. If it goes through the nose, it is called an NG tube. N is for nasal. Because of his midline cleft, Peter's nose opened to his mouth. We threaded the tube through the bit of nasal tissue that formed a partial nostril, and GI jokingly called it an OG/NG tube. GI has a unique cache of inside jokes.

Hours after getting home, the boxes arrived. Many boxes arrived. I did not recognize everything in these boxes. What are they for? We pulled out a 60ml syringe and another NG tube for when he would spit up the one currently installed. The nurse trained Kyle to put it back. It was too much for me.

This was home.

But, he grew worse.

It was not working. The food was too much. The pain was too much. It was terrible to hear how he choked and gagged after eating. My body stiffened to the sound of his suffering, holding him on my lap as I sat on the rocking chair.

After a sleepless and heavily documented week, I returned with Peter to the dreaded place for a one-week follow-up. My aunt accompanied me because I did not want to drive by myself. I waited in a room for Dr. Posner with Peter, Aunt Corrine and a large kangaroo on the wall.

In minute detail, I presented my spreadsheet of the events of the past week: the volume taken in, the volume vomited out, the diapers, the types of pain, the crying and the heartache.

In the week he was home, the GI clinic's scales told us, his weight remained the same. My aunt sat in the corner behind me. Dr. Posner leaned towards me, locked eyes with me, and said, "That you have written all this shows us you are doing everything you can. Let us help take some of this stress for you. Let us help you carry this."

I will trust her forever for saying those words…and meaning them.

Dear Peter,

I had another vision. Christ sat with me outside the house inside the city walls. He remained with us. He would walk with us. He would journey with us. This was our Lent.

We came back. Labs revealed your sodium was really low. With a gasp, barely breathing, tears fell as I gripped the side of the crib where you lay to keep myself upright, "I didn't know…I would have taken him…I would have taken him." Transport rushed you down to the PICU.

It was my fault. I knew you were dehydrated. We tried unfortified breast milk to help, even though they told me to fortify it. My milk should have fixed you.

And here we are again, two weeks later. It is after Easter, now. Your nutrients are infused through IV. It was not my fault, because even with the very best stuff, the stuff made from my body, your little body could not handle it. The gut has to be rehabilitated, they explained. You could not gain weight without enough sodium. You gained a pound in just a few days. You weigh more now than you ever weighed before. You are two and a half months old.

And now, what will we face? At one time the cleft appeared so big. Now, it is nothing. At one time the loss of breastfeeding felt so big. What do we have now? You.

We have you.

✝✝✝

Summer and Maggie from the Palliative Care Team introduced themselves to me as I sat on my bed by the window in the hospital room, staring into the distance. They were both tall. Summer was slender with long flaxen hair and impeccable style, white cotton blouse and brown leather boots, chic and relaxed. Her intent look overshadowed Maggie's presence. The clinical control of her voice and empathic nods invited me to share.

Absorbed in my feelings, my grief and my worry, my thoughts spilled out, "If it continues like this... if any more time that passes that he doesn't gain weight, that is like still losing weight. Then at some point—" I cut myself off, shaking my head to stop the thoughts, "I shouldn't be thinking about this."

Summer invited me not to push away the thoughts. "Maybe the fact that this is on your mind tells you this is what you need to be thinking about." *Who is this?* She walked in as everyone walks in, but Summer walked in like light coming in through a window. She spoke to me and looked at me. I could say anything to her.

That day or the next, the decision was made. A semi-permanent central line catheter, called a Broviac, would be tunneled through Peter's chest and inserted into his superior vena cava. Now he would get his nutrition intravenously, not just temporarily, but semi-permanently. While he is under general anesthesia, the doctors will also poke a G-tube button through his abdominal wall like an earring through an ear. I hate that Cally was right.

Dear Peter,

The question of what could have happened stayed before me when your sodium went too high. We made an advance directive for you. Around the conference table, with Kyle by my side for a family meeting, I decided, "Whatever you can do, we want you to try. Even if there is just a 10% chance, we want you to try."

We did not need to discuss it. How I said those words; I will never know; how I could answer that question, quietly but firmly, no matter what, we would do everything we could to save you.

And that is what we are doing. The future is uncertain. But no matter what, we will do everything we can for you. We will face whatever comes. You are my son. You are loved. You are wanted. We will take care of you.

†††

In the PICU again, Winnie, his night nurse who wears flamboyant tights and a dyed-red pixie cut, convinced me to sleep at Family House, a long-term residential facility for families with children in the hospital. Peter would be hungry and up all night preparing for anesthesia the next day. A Lyft car drove me across town to its own location where the children's hospital used to be. Pictorial Victorians lined the roadway as we drove alongside Golden Gate Park. Inside Family House, up the ancient elevator, the little room's window opened to a vertical tunnel through which I could listen to the conversations in the kitchen. Three beds crowded a hot room with cracked walls. The bathroom was just outside the door, shared by someone who did not regularly put the toilet lid down.

Nevertheless, I slept.

A Lyft car delivered me back to the hospital in the morning in time to see Peter's crib and Peter rolled out of the room, down to the second floor for surgery. My phone pinged, "I know" a recording of James' voice set as the text message alert. Brian was outside.

I rushed down and cried for a moment at the sight of my old friend of 14 years who went to the military and back and now lived in San Francisco. The comfort of seeing someone I knew showered over me. He was familiar. It was a piece of home and heart. Someone you could hug. He fitted a helmet on my head. Jumping on the back of his motorcycle, I ran away.

He drove us to Treasure Island. Riding across the Bay Bridge like this was terrifying. His once-broken ribs suffered from my grip.

To my mind, Treasure Island is a mystical place from Robert Louis Stevenson's imagination made real by a Disney movie. The West Coast has its own man-made Treasure Island created for the Golden Gate International Exposition in 1939, built on the rubbish of the 1906 fire.

From there you can view the uninterrupted skyline of San Francisco. The view awoke love for the city in me. We explored deserted Navy barracks and sat on rocks to talk and muse. My focus broke up randomly. He understood because old friends do.

Brian chauffeured me across the bridge and across town to the beach, the happily neglected part of the much gentrified San Francisco. It presented like any beach town in California. Meandering across the sand in black suede ankle boots, I witnessed the expansiveness of the ocean. My lungs opened to breathe deeper in that moment than they had in the last month...or two.

I searched the sand for treasures to bring my children: a broken ruffled shell, a sand dollar, another sand dollar, and crab claws. Crab cadavers were sprinkled across the sand. Nature happens. Only when I looked back at Brian did I realize he has not followed me. He stood back, observing, laughing at the child-like wonder in the woman he met when we kids starting out on life. It was that sense of wonder which made us friends in the first place. Brian stepped forward to join me, looking visually dissonant in this scene with his height, weight and bulky leather jacket.

"What is it about the ocean?" I mused.

"It's that it's so powerful, you can get lost in it and just give up all your control," he answered.

Not for me, no, "It's that it never changes. It keeps going...just goes on forever...it keeps going." Dr. John Buri referenced the waves of life in my undergraduate psychology courses at the University of St. Thomas. Sometimes they fall gentle and easy, but wait long enough and they will throw you about. Wait a little longer, and they subside, the tide withdraws.

For the first time since we arrived in San Francisco, I felt hope.

The seashells and my wooden rosary brighten the indigo terrazzo shelf in Peter's room. It was my place, with stacks of art and architecture books from home and Christopher's Books, a locally owned bookshop on Potrero Hill. It was the fruit of my discovery, the fruit of my walks.

The next night my family arrived. Brian spread out chicken, fruit and coconut Labne from the Farmer's Market to Family House, obtained by bartering the whole rotisserie chickens he cooks for his bread. At dusk, we rambled about Golden Gate Park. Spying a bookstore, Green Apple Books, we browsed inside. Kyle hung back while Brian interviewed the children. I spied a coloring book based on *The Little Prince*. Kyle offered to buy it for me.

In *The Little Prince*, a pilot crash-lands in the desert. He is running out of water and must repair his airplane. There in the desert, isolated from the world, he encounters the Little Prince alone in the desert. The Little Prince shares with the pilot his journey across the universe and his strange encounters. The pilot wants to survive the desert. He wants to leave. The Little Prince demands his attention, asking him questions, telling him stories, but never satisfying the pilot's burning curiosity of this strange being from Asteroid B-612.

"If you want a friend, tame me," the fox told to the Prince[1] while he searches Earth for friendship. The fox of-

---

[1] Antoine de Saint-Exupery, *The Little Prince*. Translated by Irene Testot-Ferry. Wordsworth Collector's Editions. (Ware, England: Wordsworth Editions, 2018).

fers an opportunity to the Little Prince to sacrifice, to give his time and energy to someone he cannot control.

During Peter's MRI, I journal:

- I feel anxious because this room is empty.
- The little fox says, "If you want a friend, tame me."
- I feel a tightness in my breath and heart
- "If you tame me, you are responsible for me."
- He is my little fox.
- I am the aviator, watching it all unfold.
- The Little Prince is beyond me, a wonder I have encountered.
- I cannot tame him. I cannot control him.
- The Little Prince is my life, this beautiful adventure.
- When it feels I must focus on important things, like preserving life.
- The Little Prince is my adventure. He is better to focus on.
- I must draw his pictures. I cannot worry about life and death.
- Right now is what matters.

Hold the Little Prince when he suffers. Draw his pictures. When the feelings arrive, stay with them. You do not have to run to them or away from them.

Chapter 6

The Finding in the Temple

When his parents saw him, they were astonished, and his mother said to him, "Son, why have you done this to us? Your father and I have been looking for you with great anxiety."

...But they did not understand what he said to them. He went down with them and came to Nazareth, and was obedient to them; and his mother kept all these things in her heart. (Luke 2: 49, 50-51)

When Peter gained enough weight, we moved out of the PICU to the Transitional Care Unit, lovingly called the T-CUP, like a dizzying Disney ride. Total Parenteral Nutrition (TPN) pumped through his Broviac into his superior vena cava to his heart with enough sodium for an adult. Breast milk ran from a bag, through his G-tube, into his stomach. As he gained, Peter grew stronger.

We learned our lesson from the last hospitalization. We created a plan. My parents watched the children while Kyle worked. On weekends, my children and husband traveled to San Francisco. We could be together. Rebecca reserved the room at Family House, my nightly escape, without an end date. The Lyft ride occupied 45 minutes in the evening. A 20-minute commute in the morning returned me to the hospital.

"Where did you walk today?" became the standard conversation starter. I memorized the shops in the Dogpatch (south on 3rd Street), the shops along Mariposa Ave (going west), the Wednesday Farmer's Market in front of Subway and Peasant Pies (north of the hospital) and the 1-mile route to the Design District. Outside on the sidewalk. I daydreamed of dressing well and drinking a cocktail at Perry's. On my first visit to the Design District, I overheard a lady raving about it when she visited. The Design Center was an art gallery of items for sale. A $300 bronze doorknob captivated me.

I could tell you the restaurants along the waterfront and the only place to get seafood. My walks lengthened.

After hiking two miles north to Market Street, I prayed a moment at St. Patrick's. Fr. Raphael, our hospital chaplain, lived there.

The church was a sanctuary from the dirty street. Homeless men, scattered among the pews, rested from the world. Kneeling before the altar, my eyes traveled upward the marble sculptures. Our Lady held the Christ Child. Just above them is the Crucifix. That is how it is, holding your child before the cross.

Anxious to keep moving, I left soon. Old Navy was one block west.

Each walk commenced at the beginning of Peter's nap. I allowed myself two to three hours away to wander. "This is my town now," I told my husband on the phone.

Every morning I ate a hard-boiled egg with salt and pepper and a bowl of oatmeal. If I successfully ordered it the night before, it waited for me when I arrived by Lyft at 7:00 or 7:30 a.m. I cart a little cooler back and forth, filled, then emptied of bags of breast milk. Those bags of mine filled the fridge in the TCUP. The nurses mentioned it daily.

Every day, Nurse Amy Chang from our care coordination team (FLIGHT) visited me, as did Peg and Rebecca. Amy and I bantered with hearty laughter, much the same with Peg. Rebecca and I discussed mental health disorders, social work versus psychology and my design passions. Dr.

Posner visited often, more and more taken with Peter. He improved and won their hearts.

Easter came a week and a half later on March 27. We abandoned our traditions and our menu to try to adapt in San Francisco. Peter had been there so long already. By the generosity of the Intercontinental Mark Hopkins Hotel, we stayed for free in a fancy hotel room for Easter.

On my half-mile walk in Union square, I purchased playful goodies at Williams-Sonoma combining retail therapy with indulgent motherhood. It all felt good.

An error in the reservation afforded me one night to stay by myself. Planning around my pumping schedule, I called a taxi downtown late in the evening. The driver taught me about jazz and the sights. He recommended the SF Jazz Center. Stunned by the elegance of the Mark Hopkins facade, I forgot to tip him on my way out.

Doormen opened magnificent ebony doors punctuated with gold and carried my luggage. I felt too grand and too small to be there. The lobby's crystal empire chandeliers glittered in gilt. The tiny elevator spoke to the history.

This was a black-and-white film.

Opening my door to two queen size beds dressed in ivory against low, wall-mounted headboards, I threw myself on one and delighted in the grandiosity of the decor. The flat screen television stood atop a cherry tone dresser. Like most hotel rooms I have seen, the square footage was cramped with furniture, but the finishes were beautiful.

The bathroom, true to 1930's scale, housed a marble pedestal sink with pronounced graining. Riding the elevator to the Top of the Mark, I explored the nightclub on the top floor. An aged couple knew their steps as a Motown band with resonant vocals engaged the diners in dancing. Across the floor, a flamboyant thirty-something-year-old man with an elongated face reveled in his olives and the music, gesturing as if the lead singer were singing to him. The waiter took for my order, "a vodka martini, please."

Caught up in the celebratory feeling, I ordered another.

Upon returning to the room, a neatly arranged tray with grapes, pears, apples and a metal tin of bittersweet chocolate nibbles sat on the dresser. Sprawled out in bed, I turned on the television and watched *13 Going on 30*, embracing the comfort I missed.

In the morning, I woke early and paid the price for drinking to excess.

Saturday, the children arrived. After the day at the hospital, we drove to the hotel. The rate for valet parking caused us to gasp, but what other choice did we have? We took the children upstairs.

It was trying to stay with five bodies in one room with a 1930's bathroom. Although cramped, we were determined to be positive! This was a gift after all. The children went to bed. Kyle and I sat on the hallway floor waiting for them to fall asleep. We filled the baskets and drank cocktails he brought from home. Then we left the baskets just outside the door for the kids to discover in the morning and went to bed. I hesitated about the plan. But Kyle reassured me, surely in a place as fancy as this, nothing will happen to those baskets.

Oh, naïve, out-of-town, small-town, country folk. The children woke, opened the door to see their baskets. "They aren't there!" Miriam cried. The baskets were gone.

I looked outside. Thinking rapidly, we told the children, "The Easter Bunny must be confused because we aren't home."

In my Easter dress, I asked for the hotel management. As we sat on the fancy couches of the hotel lobby, I explained how we set baskets out and implored, "Do you know why we're here?" *Do you know we are the family you donated a room for because my kid is in the hospital? How much can I say without telling you how devastated I feel?*

"Yes," she knew and she sincerely apologized. She would send security to search the halls and offered to put together a basket with sweets. With a knock at the door, she snuck a large basket with cookies, candies and teddy bears to me. A few minutes later, she returned to say the security guard located the kids' baskets on a different floor. We repeated our tale about the Easter Bunny's confusion.

We crowded into St. Dominic's, 15 minutes before mass started. A gentleman, who just opened the choir loft, invited families to ascend the staircase. From the mountaintop, we kneeled and saw that resplendent edifice with its woodcarvings along the walls and intricate, stained-glass windows. How much better than the Top of the Mark! My soul throbbed as it soared throughout the liturgy.

I tried to be positive, but my heart was broken. For whatever we did with the kids to make the day feel like Easter, it was incomplete. Peter was not with us. The rest of the day blurred in the tiredness. I was tired of trying, tired of pretending we could make this day anything other than a vague spiritual reference to the meaning of it all. Easter passed. After two nights of using an ice chest for the children's dinner table, the children and Kyle left and Peter and I remained.

Alone again, I familiarized myself with the hospital's
Center for Families on the 6th floor. An unremarkable
room, obscure books lined the shelves to the left of the entrance. Visitors are asked to sign in where Lisa Lee greets
them sympathetically. She has been there before. Her long,
bright red curls filled my sight and made her unforgettable.
The center offered magazines to borrow, free tasteless coffee and shoulder massages on Wednesdays. The volunteer
who massages shoulders inquires who you are there for and
why they are there. The time I said I did not want to talk, my
shoulder massage ended a couple minutes early. The time I
answered, I felt my whole body tense up.

To find peace, I walked three miles to the Ferry Building
hoping to rent a bike halfway. The bike rental shop was
closed. Burned by the sun, I purchased sunflowers from the
Tuesday Farmer's Market and an aqua dessert bowl from
Heath Ceramics to hold my seashells.

My feet ached as I walked back. A stranger walked ahead
of me with a large remote control car under his arm. Fixed
on his car, I fantasized about sitting on top of it as it drove
down the sidewalk. Blisters formed on the balls of my feet. I
hailed a cab.

The flowers helped to bring peace, but they are not a ne-
cessity. Still, I appreciated the spark of joy as I fit them into
a plastic pitcher on the wide graphite windowsill.

Fr. Raphael shared in his homily about his experiences
caring for the livestock in his native country. He looked after
nearly 100 animals and sometimes drove them for miles to
find green grass or water for their day. He ate once a day.
One day, when he was 25, a lion attacked one of the cows.
As the warrior of the community, he could not just sit idly
by. So knowing the tricks and techniques, he killed that lion.

Then he said, "That's what the Good Shepherd will do for you."

We told the kids we would celebrate Regina's birthday on Saturday, April 9th. Her birthday was Friday. We avoided the truth to avoid a lie. Throughout the 8th, I shared pictures of Regina with visitors and watched videos of her.

Three weeks after Easter, the conversation shifted.

A doctor introduced the idea first.

But how? How could we go home? Looking up and down the medical pole which held pump after pump, I had my doubts. *How could I manage that with a baby and pumping and three other kids?*

Sharon was Peter's nurse that day. In her forties with decades of experience, Sharon knew nursing at a deeper level than the young ones. Her hair is brown and shoulder length. Her frame is soft enough to be motherly and comforting. Confiding my thoughts to her, she said matter-of-factly, "Oh you'll be able to. The home pumps are really small. They fit in a little backpack. You'll be able to go to the park."

Just like that, she made the impossible possible.

The teaching began. Nurse after nurse explained Broviac care and g-tube volume and rates. We practiced connecting and disconnecting the Broviac: take an alcohol wipe and scrub for ten seconds, dry for ten seconds, flush 10ml of saline, scrub for ten, dry for ten, connect TPN tubing. We learned dressing changes, cap changes, and lab draws.

A woman from Coram came to teach us. She coined strange phrases like, "You want to go to Disneyland, take off Mickey's ear" and "I don't know what this is for; you just pull it off." She described her method of priming as "genius."

Because of our health insurance and Peter's specialty care, Home Health Nursing and training was not an option. The doctors created a plan for us to go to Family House and spend a few days close to the hospital to make sure we were comfortable with the things we learned.

"So—do you want to go home?" Dr. Duncan Henry asked with a grin as he walked in. Such momentous words said so simply.

Panic set in. The nurse, Caroline, and Dr. Henry deliberated. They recommended Peter stay another night. "Go back to Family House, have dinner, enjoy the free babysitting," Dr. Henry encouraged us.

Holistic medicine. For the first time in over a month, Kyle and I would be alone together. We spent the evening at Family House. A lamb gyro made dinner for me. From the corner dive, Kyle bought a Jenny burger.

Our confidence returned in the morning with the new plan. Rather than learn lab draws, dressing changes and how to operate the TPN and G-tube pumps, Peter and I would drive in each week to be taught by the Infusion Center nurses. Yes, I agreed, anything to get us home.

The man from Transport wheeled me in a wheelchair with Peter in my arms. You aren't allowed to walk out on your feet with the baby. Kyle followed with the luggage. My little son looked just a little bigger than before. My thoughts dared to whisper, *what a triumph this is*.

We were leaving.

A part of me thought we would never leave. We rode down the elevator, through the lobby, and into the light-filled foyer.

We won...we did it, I reflected, staring into his eyes. This was his biggest moment yet. He survived.

Karen from Coram sent a different woman to Family House who might make more sense to help us connect Peter to his TPN. She arrived at 4 p.m. and articulated long directions clearly. By 7 p.m. I could think of nothing but food.

The connection was successful. We fumbled around in the morning but managed.

With a borrowed stroller, we three walked to the Botanical Gardens in Golden Gate Park. His little pump that fit into a basket sat in the bottom bin of the stroller. We went to the park, just as Sharon said. I fretted over his tubes as images of the stroller wheels catching them flashed in my mind.

After my first visit alone with Peter to the Infusion Center, the reality of a new dawn settled in our lives, and my heart overflowed with words on the turns of Interstate 580.

✝✝✝

The nightmare transitioned into a dream.
It was dark and foggy,
Felt like there was no way out.
I could no longer breathe.
The tears kept coming but would not stop
The night transitioned to a dream.

I saw a light come down upon me.
A breath of air filled up my lungs.
Through the clouds saw the break of day.
The night transitioned in a way.

I kept on walking; I could not stop.
In these forced steps I had to move.
Until I saw your eyes light up,
And night transitioned into you

I saw you grow and gain and thrive.
    Then I knew you were alive.
My son, my love, my little one,
Now in my view, I see the sun.
On we walked, untied and free,
My little one and me.
My feet on the ground, I could breathe again.
The nightmare was at an end.

The place became the place for me
when again I could see
How to love and how to be
with you, my little one and me

The nightmare ended, though still, I fear
That if I turn around its near.
I could lose what we have gained
It will never be the same.
I see a reminder in those here
Who walked with me and held my hand,
Making it possible to stand,
I breathe again, I see the sky,
know that morning is drawing nigh.

Part II

The Luminous Mysteries

Chapter 7

The Baptism at the Jordan

He was still speaking when, behold, a bright cloud overshadowed them, and a voice from the cloud said, "This is my beloved Son, with whom I am well pleased." (Matthew 17:5)

We were home. But what did that mean? Mara, a repeat and favorable nurse from our last hospital day, organized our boxes for us with neatly handwritten labels listing their contents. Arriving home, I knew what I needed and where it was. How different from our acclimation before.

The new routine began. We hit our stride during that month with weekly labs, weekly weight checks, weekly dressing changes, daily TPN and continuous g-tube feeds. I changed my job title to "stay-at-home-mother" to manage it all. A handful of events colored the calendar pages: dinner at the Otts, the Fruit and Nut Festival, a Mother's Day tea party at home. We went blueberry picking. The children buried Peter with toys in his bouncer, initiating him into their tribe.

One month later, Peter was not himself. At the Emergency Department, labs revealed his potassium was too low. After a dose of potassium in Modesto, we took our first helicopter ride.

One step at a time, I whispered to myself.

This is really happening.

Was my child ill enough to use the helicopter?

The pilot reviewed the risks. "First," he said, "we could crash." He paused, "Lastly...don't touch the buttons."

I did not touch the buttons.

A helicopter lifted up with tremendous strength like a giant elevator. Holding tight to the air in my lungs, a panic attack was just around the corner. Every time inhaling slowly, to prevent the breath from becoming a full-blown hyperventilating breath, I declared to myself: "It's an adventure!"

The view below us revealed homes I never knew existed nestled between enchanted foothills dividing our valley from one of the richest parts of the country. Without a mid-air sense of direction, the towns below were unrecognizable.

The pilot told me the names of towns in sight. He checked periodically on if I was okay. As the helmet pinned my earrings against my neck and the foreign microphone reach in front of me threateningly, my mind wrapped around my voice enveloping me in the silence where reflections flourish. To his inquiries, I only nodded. Strapped to a gurney between two nurses dressed in navy flight suits, Peter slept.

We landed on the roof of Benioff Children's Hospital. The air whipped my skirt around as I made my descent. We were here.

In April, Family House's long-promised move opened a new location a mere four blocks from the hospital. The morning and evening commute with Lyft drivers was at an end. The distanced furnished my day with two guaranteed walks. A streamlined modern ascetic defined the new building, more hotel than house.

Orange laser cut metal embellished the white and orange flat-faced facade rising up from 4th street and Mission Bay Blvd North. On the second floor of the u-shaped building, in place of the forlorn fire escape of the Koret Family House, this Grand Family House boasted a courtyard with actual plants, barbeques and outdoor seating.

After sharing a bathroom with strangers, telling a disoriented kid he was in the wrong room in the middle of the night and listening to people talk in the kitchen through my window, the refuge of privacy relieved my heartache.

In that place, I left the hospital behind. If I wanted company, I lingered near the front desk to chat with Anna or Sarah between phone calls at the front desk. On other days, I sought solitude in the silence of my lonely room. I entered the code on the keypad, and as the two heavy glass doors opened before me, I passed through, eyes downcast, shoulders slumped under the weight of my bag and Peter's condition, and my face expression a bit blank, an expression like many other parents. Every bit of me cried from the inside, "It was a hard day."

Anna asked how I was. With tears, I shrugged, "okay." She understood, stood up to hug me, then left me alone. The nightly promenade, a television binge and conversation with Kyle, sustained my strength. Here it was home, not my home, but home enough to recover and prepare for another day at the hospital.

Over the course of six days, Peter's electrolytes returned to their right range. Discharge instructions remained the same: if he spikes a fever, we must return to rule-out the possibility of an infection in his line. During teachings, staff continued to lay upon us warnings to be careful, quick and sterile when we change his Broviac cap. At each cap change, I stared down through that tiny opening as a portal of death, seeing, with my mind's eye, germs and bacteria fighting to get in.

Peter's fever brought us back again. This time, there was no room at the Inn; all the beds at UCSF were full. At 1 a.m., an ambulance delivered Peter and me to Children's Hospital Oakland, CHO for short. In their Emergency Dept., I wept for want of sleep. Peter could no longer sleep comfortably in my arms. He was "hospital trained." So he cried.

"Do you want me to bring a bassinet for him?" the nurse asked.

Yes, I agreed and, desperately, I drifted to sleep. An intercom interrupted that repose multiple times each hour.

When two hours passed, they moved us to the "party room" where five other patients slept. Still and silent when we arrived, after two hours, the noise began. With the curtain partition closed around us, the sunless shadow and exhaustion drained my spirits. Their medical inquiries met with my short and rude answers.

Only the bustling hallway during Peter's nap provided an escape from the enveloping noise and darkness. The fluorescent lights brightened the old taupe floors and walls that dress so many hospitals unbecomingly. This was not home. This was not my place.

Twelve hours at CHO passed like three days. Sympathetic doctors moved us to a private little room in the NICU that we might find some quiet. "Didn't it make more sense to move people who weren't used to hospital life?" I wondered.

"No, we moved you because you spend so much time in the hospital." Sunshine streamed in the little room from a wide window at the top of the wall. There was room enough for the hospital crib, sleeper chair and my suitcase. It may have only been a few feet larger than my partitioned place in the party room, but the light expanded the walls into a space where I could breathe.

The nurse and I built rapport talking about UCSF's acquisition of CHO and how it affected staff dynamics.

"Is it safe to walk this neighborhood?" I posed.

"Yes—" she outlined my route.

Head up and shoulders back, I sauntered out. A few feet outside the NICU doors, I turned back to ask, "Which way did you say?" Cheerfully, she mocked my confident strut.

It was beautiful out, not too hot, not too cold. The directions led me under the overpass and out into the shopping center. At Walgreens, pampering purchases added up to needed toiletries, pads and lipstick. Along a chain link fence, from alternating pink and white petals a chartreuse stamen stuck out from violet whiskers. I captured it with my camera to give it to Miriam and apply to a watercolor experiment. Shining brightly, the sun warmed my skin through the cool breeze. *This could be my town, too. I can do this. I can adapt.*

As the sun began to set in our little room, I dressed for bed. There was a knock at the door. The nurse told me transport was on the way. Smiling with a renewed optimism, I slipped back into day-clothes again.

The theme of the "desert" frequented conversations with Summer. First as the desert from *The Little Prince*; then later, the spiritual desert. During the formative years of early adolescence, I read *A Story of a Soul*, the autobiography of St. Therese of Lisieux. Early in her life, the desert represented a place of longing, a place to be with God. It was Mount Carmel where hermits first gathered to pray, as told in the history of the Carmelite order. It was the place where Therese and her sisters would one day enter.

She wrote, "I remember that I said once that I should like to go with you to a far-off desert, and you said that you felt the same, but would wait until I was big enough."[1]

It was isolating but not barren because there, in the desert, away from the distraction of the world, one encountered God.

"One does not go into the desert to leave something – the noise, the world, occupations -- one goes there above all to find something, rather Someone. One does not go alone to find oneself, to put oneself in contact with one's inner self, as in so many forms of non-Christian meditation. To be alone with oneself can mean to find oneself with the worst of company. The believer goes into the desert, goes down into his own heart, to renew his contact with God, because he knows that 'Truth dwells in the interior man'"[2]

As a child, I wondered what my desert would be.

Now I wondered about the big picture. *What is this all about: Peter's life and his health issues?*

It invited comparison to hiking through the desert, as I did at 18, outside Las Vegas. Our team of missionaries moved down the wild path, combing through gangly desert trees in the warmth of a Nevada February. After hours, we rounded some bare bushes and came to a clearing. There we saw a waterfall.

That night, as I quitted the hospital room with a walk to Family House from UCSF and not CHO as expected, I saw

---

[1] St. Thérèse of Lisieux. *The Story of a Soul.* Edited by Mother Agnes of Jesus. Translated by Michael Day. (Rockford, Illinois: Tan Books and Publishers, 1997), 36.

[2] Fr. Reniero Cantalamessa, "1st Lent Homily, 2014." https://www.ewtn.com/catholicism/library/1st-lent-homily-2014-3202

how these hospitalizations renewed my relationship with God through the solitude and acute moments of insecurity that demanded trust. Christ went out to the desert to pray. Hermits gathered on Mount Carmel. Therese was hidden from the world. The desert is isolation, dryness, a place without consolation. It is a word for the Dark Night of the Soul, where one's trust in God is put to the test away from the consolations that distract us from healing. Jesus left the desert to be baptized and begin his public ministry.

Summer and I discussed the need to prepare my backpack for a journey into the desert, to take what I need to survive.

This was Peter's life so far: a lot of desert.

It was a lot of walking in the heat, treading through rocks and dried up brush, lost.

After my exhaustion reached its peak, suddenly, there appeared his enormous cleft smile for the first time, his face so full of joy.

It was unbelievable.

His smile carried the power of encountering the magnificent Burney Falls at our annual hiking spot and in my dreams as an adult. Yet, this was unmistakably a desert waterfall.

Just as joyful, but beautiful because it was his cleft smile.

There are these hidden treasures in the desert, like holding onto the vision of a flowering meadow one sees below the mountain at one end of the switch back. I can choose to stay with that vision. This was his first smile.

Before that moment, my water was running low.

Like the Little Prince, he led me to the well.

In the lab's petri dish, his blood culture grew yeast. For his second surgery, the pediatric surgery team would remove the Broviac they placed during the first surgery. This time, I carried him to the second floor operating room. Holding my breath, I handed him off to the nurse. Slowly, I returned to his empty room and waited. My heart grew braver.

Using *20 Ways to Draw a Tulip* for inspiration, I painted flowers with a travel watercolor set from Arch Supplies and drew a sketch of Peter. Jane, the day's resident, and I laughed over my attempt.

When transport brought a sleeping Peter back to the room, I cherished the sight of his chest without the Tegaderm dressing distracting from his beauty.

In two weeks, his antibiotic course was completed. Cultures were clear. They replaced the Broviac: his third surgery.

July at home was a golden month. It was a honeymoon.

TPN volume: down.

Volume of breast milk tolerated through the g-tube: up.

Bottle-feeding: good.

Weight gain: up.

The doctor showed me a spot on the growth chart. He was back on the chart; the dots marched straight up.

Kyle and I celebrated our seventh wedding anniversary in small ways and with bittersweet chocolate cake. He gave me Swarovski crystal earrings, the same design as a pair of diamond earrings I had swooned over in Tiffany's window at Union square, a triangle of clear sparkling mesh. As a gift to myself, inspired by quotes shared online, I bought *A Call to a Deeper Love: The Family Correspondence of the Parents of Saint Therese of the Child Jesus.*

To celebrate the date of my birth, July 27th, I breezed into the trendy wine bar, Camp 4, to meet two former coworkers, Tori and Lauren. They presented a huge bouquet of jewel tone dahlias to me. Earlier that week, I said I never buy flowers for myself, though I wanted to badly. My friends remembered. They bought me flowers.

Then July ended.

I was pregnant.

Chapter 8

The Wedding at Cana

His mother said to the servants, "Do whatever he tells you." Now standing there were six stone water jars for the Jewish rites of purification, each holding twenty or thirty gallons. Jesus said to them, "Fill the jars with water." And they filled them up to the brim. (John 2: 5-7)

August 2

Dear Camille,

This morning has been a rough one. I talked with the doctors, hoping Peter would be okay. Yesterday, during the "Hail Holy Queen," the reference to life as a "valley of tears" stayed with me. In St. Zélie Martin's letters,[1] she writes that we are fooling ourselves if we think this life is for our enjoyment. The thought of what she suffered (four of her children dying, three as infants, one at age 5) and how she persevered, has taken on a life of its own inside my heart. I look at her experience, pondering it. Even after her last baby died, named Thérèse, she said she wanted to have another—to have another Thérèse. And look what happened! God gave her another Thérèse, whom a Pope called one of the greatest saints of modern times. Zélie died before she could see the fruit of what she suffered.

We are suffering now.

---

[1] Zélie and Louis Martin, *A Call to a Deeper Love: The Family Correspondence of the Parents of St. Thérèse of the Child Jesus 1863-1885.* Edited by Dr. Frances Renda. Translated by Anne Connors Hess (New York: St. Paul's, 2011).

I measure the image of her writing that letter as she prayed for another Thérèse against the fear I have with Peter…the fear that I will walk in the room one day and things will not be okay…that at any moment it could all disappear.

With the others, there might have been one midnight check the first time they slept through the night, but no more after that.

I lay awake and think of Peter, wondering if he is moving.

There was one positive reflection yesterday. As is my nature, I am very driven at everything I do. If I were not having more children, striving to adapt and thrive despite all the difficulty, what would I drive at?

Material gain? More vanity? What would all that effort be worth in the end?

I guess, if this is what God wants, it is better this way.

The thought brought some relief, anyway.

— Kathryn

The *Catechism of the Catholic Church* teaches us about the Communion of Saints.

"When the Lord comes in glory, and all his angels with him, death will be no more and all things will be subject to him. But at the present time, some of his disciples are pilgrims on the earth. Others have died and are being purified, while still others are in glory, contemplating in full light, God himself triune and one, exactly as he is…So it is that the union of the wayfarers with the brethren who sleep in the peace of Christ is in no way interrupted, but on the contrary, according to the constant faith of the Church, this union is reinforced by an exchange of spiritual goods... Being more closely united to Christ, those who dwell in heaven fix the whole Church more firmly in holiness...They do not cease to intercede with the Father for us."[2]

Zélie's daughter had an ear infection. It was the end of the 19th century. Without antibiotics, the doctors were powerless. Zélie described the odorous, draining pus. The girl lost her hearing. When Zélie prayed to her deceased son in Heaven, the ear was miraculously cured!

On an August night, as I drove down the roomy lanes of Christofferson Blvd to take Peter to Turlock's Emergency Department, I prayed, "Be with me, Zélie."

St. Therese walked beside me as I walked with God. At one time every book about her lived on my shelves. My only impression of her parents came from *The Story of a Soul*. The letters between mother and father in *A Call to a Deeper Love* were my comfort this season.

Zélie was an ordinary woman, overwhelmed with her work but driven to press on. She longed to have her children near her but felt exhausted when they were. She was profoundly attached to her husband.

It seemed God protected us from fully feeling the heat of the fire we endured. In those days of reflection, I began to understand how very bad things were in the early months of Peter's life.

Zélie lost four of her children. There were no vaccines and no antibiotics. One child died at 7 weeks. After a healthy

---

[2] Catholic Church. *Catechism of the Catholic Church*. 2nd ed. (Huntingdon, PA: Our Sunday Visitor, 2000), §§ 954-6.

birth, Zélie could not produce enough milk to nourish her. They sent the child to a wet nurse, and she improved immediately only to decline again. Marie, the eldest, observed the baby's crying and suspected the infant was starving. When Zélie brought the baby home, it was too late. She died of starvation.

That was my Peter.

My Peter was dying of starvation.

Modern medicine could have saved that baby because it saved my Peter.

Headlines informed me of the trials of the Syrian refugees. They emigrate for their lives. Mothers choose to leave their ten-year-old boys because a ten-year-old boy is more likely to survive on his own. The mother must make a choice. No homes, no beds, babies born in boats, fleeing the violence only to find more when they were placed in Syrian slums ruled by the radical Muslims they were fleeing. Their suffering is great.

On August 4, John Vianney's feast day, I thought of our first child, miscarried, and named John Marie in memory of John and Mary who stood at the foot of the cross. Such a name indirectly made St. Vianney his patron.

"Please, heal Peter and keep our unborn baby safe and healthy. Let it be as healthy, physically and mentally, as our other children," I pray to him and our other miscarried baby, Paul Joseph.

In the past, I had heard women react negatively to the common response to the question of the baby's sex: "We don't care as long as it's healthy!"

They thought the speaker implied if the baby were not healthy they would not want it. It seemed a silly conversation to me as I sat in the hospital with one baby on the monitors and another under my heart. Having a baby with severe medical needs, with surgeries and never-ending fears is an awful thing. Admitting its difficulty does not diminish the baby's beauty or worth of the baby. It is good to think and pray for the health of our babies. Nothing is guaranteed.

To practice gratitude, I scribbled a list of the things that fell into place to prepare me for this hospitalization. God prepared me thus:

- Manicured nails
- These reflections I had on accepting our situation
- Therapy time with Summer
- A pleasant morning energy
- Finished chores around the house
- Downtime spent with the kids
- I felt sweet towards Kyle

The report came quickly: another line infection. Treatment followed as before. Two surgeries: Broviac out, Broviac in, with a bunch of antibiotics in between.

The doctors look for nothing new to grow in the blood cultures. One blood culture was drawn daily. Once three days are clear, we wait for the course of antibiotics to complete. At that time, the expert Infectious Disease team approved Peter's cleft lip repair to go forward as planned on August 10th.

On the "Cleft Mommies" Facebook group, women wrote that they cried when they saw their babies' changed faces.

That night I said goodbye to his sweet face. The tears refused to stay as I kissed his enormous cleft, that prominent hole. When we put his blanket over his head, he reminded

me of E.T. With love we made many jokes. His little lip flaps
opened when he smiled, laughed or cried. Now, those en-
dearing things would be gone.

What will he look like? I kissed his cheeks, aware that after
this, it will forever be different.

My heart ached just as much when I handed Peter to the
nurse on the second floor. This time, Kyle was with me.

Waiting anxiously, we ate sushi, walked around and
stared at our laptops in Peter's empty room. Hours later, the
call finally came. After calling once earlier, they forgot to call
again. Peter was awake.

Energy pulsed through my legs as I rushed to the elevator to go to the second-floor lobby. My mind swarmed with
the obsession to get there. Nothing else existed. I must hold
him again.

Checking with the front desk of a darkened lobby, a
nurse walked us back to the end of the row of stalls, curtains, and recovering kids.

In the crib, searching for his face amidst the bundle of
blankets, I laid eyes on him.

He was beautiful!

With a gasp, new tears fell.

This face with his little nose and beautiful cheeks was
how God made him to be. By bringing together the separated upper lip, his nose now stuck out like a little button. His
cheeks pulled up into pillows worthy of baby's face.

A plastic surgeon did not change him. Dr. Hoffman only
made him more of who God meant him to be. God meant
him to have a nose, and now he has one. We never hid from
ourselves the reality that something went wrong in Peter's
development. Today, through the tears, something went
right.

Peter's blood cultures remained clear, the antibiotic treatment completed and doctors planned discharge. While bustling around packing up the remnants of our weeks in the hospital, I paused to use the bathroom.

Blood.

We accepted this pregnancy, though we did not want this pregnancy. I experienced only one cycle before it happened. Peter turned six months before the test read positive. Every day I hoped it would go away. Every day I tried to align my will with God's will and embrace the reality of this child.

My heart cried, "No!"

Peter lay in his crib. Opening the door, I walked out his door to the nurse's station, went on one knee beside Megan, the charge nurse, with a plan to whisper calmly to her "I think I am having a miscarriage" and then ask for help. Instead, I went on one knee, fell into her arms and bawled, "I think I am having a miscarriage!"

She sprang to nurse-like action discreetly directing other nurses to take steps. The only wheelchair in the unit was child-size. Nurses debated where to take me. Megan rushed me to the triage on the 3rd floor of the Betty Irene Moore Women's Hospital, connected to the Children's Hospital. We passed Dr. Rosenthal, a GI attending doctor with a scruffy voice and scruffier attitude. Wishing to hide from him, I shielded my face with my hand. My pregnancy was too vulnerable, and I looked ridiculous scrunched in a child-size wheelchair.

Megan brought me to the examination room. She left to find my purse so I could contact Kyle. Upon examination, the doctor found bleeding but nothing more. The cervix was closed. It was not yet possible to tell if it was a miscarriage.

With the doppler, the sound of baby's heartbeat filled the room. She directed me to rest and follow-up with my doctor.

I sat on the bed alone waiting for the doctor to return. Kyle was home. Someone from the T-CUP already called him. We talked quietly and quickly, then got off the phone. Peg stopped by because Summer was unavailable. She accompanied me back to Peter's room in the Children's Hospital.

Peter and I drove home. It was the end of August.

Triumph filled with tears. A full cup of suffering. A full cup of confusion.

St. Therese wrote to her sister, "You made me bring Daddy's tumbler and put it by the side of my thimble. You filled them both with water and asked me which was fuller. I told you they were both full to the brim and that it was impossible to put more water in them than they could hold. And so, Mother darling, you made me understand that in heaven God will give His chosen their fitting glory and that the last will have no reason to envy the first."

The bleeding slowed to spotting. Miriam came with me to the local follow-up appointment. Dr. Pheffer said calculatingly, "You know the fetus is viable?"

Yes.

He might have said, "Your baby is alive."

My heart and body jumped to defend the child inside me. I heard the heartbeat again. Pheffer's parting advice was "Avoid working too hard."

My activity slowed to a stop to make the spotting go away.

The tears were a sign to me. Not only did I accept this baby, I wanted this baby.

Chapter 9

The Proclamation of the Kingdom of God

Thomas said to him, "Master, we do not know where you are going; how can we know the way?" Jesus said to him, "I am the way and the truth and the life. No one comes to the Father except through me. (John 14:5-6)

"That same evening, when the sun appeared to be sinking into the vast stretch of the waters beyond a golden path of light, I went with you to sit upon a lonely rock. I gazed for ages on this path of light, and you said it was an image of the path to Heaven when grace lights up the way."[1]

Peter's energy was low. During our outing, I thought, *how strangely calm he is.* He spat up once in the car. His eyes sunk in. At lunch, Kyle and I discussed the symptoms and put the clues together. Something was wrong.

His local pediatrician, Dr. Li, could ease the process of getting labs. The Turlock Pediatric nurse said there was an opening in 25 minutes. It takes 15 minutes to get there. My dad said I could drop the children off at my parents. My husband rushed to shoe and load up the children while I prepared the diaper bag. Packing did not enter my mind. Getting there was the only act in front of me.

In the hallway of Turlock Pediatrics, we sat Peter on the baby scale and the nurse checked his temperature: 99.2 axil-

---

[1] St. Thérèse of Lisieux, *The Story of a Soul.* Edited by Mother Agnes of Jesus. Translated by Michael Day. (Rockford, Illinois: Tan Books and Publishers, 1997), 32.

lary. When it is that high, it must be checked more accurately. The result: 102.

In shock and anger, I muttered, "Damn it."

The thoughts came as a flood. *This means San Francisco…this means leaving home…this means being torn apart…this means returning to the desert where we seem to live half the time…this means suffering…this means making arrangements.*

We were off to the Emergency Dept. at Emmanuel Medical Center. Kyle took down my list by the phone on what to pack. He delivered my suitcase to our isolated room.

Then the nurse brought news that we would fly to San Francisco. The suitcase must be left behind in order to minimize weight on the helicopter.

This means it gets complicated.

What were my options? Could I go without him in the car?

If I have the van in San Francisco and it sits unused for two weeks, that burdens life for everyone else. Caregivers of my children need the van.

After blubbering on the phone with Dr. Henry, he said they will try to make a way for me to have a break. *What did he mean?* Dr. Posner and I spoke. She explained. She and Dr. Henry wanted to make a way for me to be able to go home for a few days while Peter is inpatient.

I protested.

Peter is very attached to me. He is eight months old.

I left eight-month-old James to return to work full-time three years ago because we needed the money. It hurt him.

I cannot do that. They are wonderful at UCSF. They love him there. But I could not take from him the stability of the person he is attached to most.

Mid-air, as I sat in the front of the helicopter with the helmet encasing my head, I heard in the headphones,

"PICU" from the flight nurse in the back.

We are in a helicopter...PICU...Is it more serious than I realize? The dazzling sun burned my face as we flew west into the evening, while the air conditioning vent directed its frozen wrath on my left leg. If I began to panic, I exhaled and replayed the cheer in my mind, "it's an adventure!" This was our second helicopter ride.

We soared up and over the clouds. Beneath us rolled a sea of them. I snapped a photograph as a mental gift for James. If, at the turn of the century St. Thérèse marveled at the elevator what would she say of this! From here I saw the golden path of light above the clouds.

Riding on the wind, we dove into the clouds. The power of the moment, the magnitude, astounded me. We sank lower. The clouds transitioned from bright white to a menacing slate gray, reminding me of the dark night, the separation from the things we love, of feeling torn from home.

We were in the dark clouds. When we passed under them, I surveyed the bay below with the sun setting before us. Along the water grew a golden path of light.

This is the way to Heaven. This way of suffering, of love, of sacrifice. *I offer this sacrifice for that young man I heard about, named Joseph, lying in critical condition because of a drunk driver.*

Earlier in the day, the Emergency Dept. nurse in Turlock asked me, "How do you do it?"

You just do. You just keep moving forward. This is the way to Heaven. To buoy us up, the Lord finds a way to light up the path, to give us hope, and keep us moving on our journey.

There are no marks on the map we use. My jittery mind, nervous and frustrated, stretched to anticipate all I could.

A man called from Emanuel Medical Center. Thick with

an Indian accent, he told me, "You need to bring Peter back to the hospital." The blood culture was positive for yeast.

"He is in the hospital. We were transferred from Emmanuel," I told him.

He should comprehend this. He was looking at the culture from weeks ago. Had they waited this long to tell us, Peter would have been dead. They did not seem to understand. They did not grasp its gravity.

It was the difference between going home and staying, possibly for weeks. It was the difference of diving into the darkness again, setting my teeth and struggling to adapt again, to make a way of life here again.

Wait and see. The future was never guaranteed. We took it for granted that we knew what would happen until something threw us off the rails and God laughed at our plans. He has something better for us. Maybe making something as simple as dinner at a table for two with my husband feel like a date.

The T-CUP at UCSF was a familiar scene. We marched in the door, through the unit, up the large elevator and through the hallway. Each room down that hallway held memories. These were my views before. Yesterday, I watched the patio on the 5th floor and other windows. Today, Mariposa Park lay before me, a place that was part of the hospital and yet separate. In the past, Family House was my peace. Then the park opened.

With anticipation, I stared as the red salvia, ceonothus, yallow, verbena, daylilies, sage, and so much more, bloomed all spring behind a chain-link fence. Fragrant, butterfly-attracting flowers filled the flower beds. The path supposedly marked the form of a butterfly wing, though it was indiscernible to me. Now that it was open, I faithfully walked the path as a way of holding Miriam close to my heart. We anticipated its opening together.

Anticipation hung on me like the fog. *What will happen? How long this time? How will we manage?* My mind spun plans and solutions repeatedly. The weight of the fabric overwhelmed me. It was better to wait and see. The view out the window at the park recalled the smell of the flowers and how it covered a multitude of smells in the city.

The fog still filled the air, but the sun would come in the afternoon. By then more would be clear. The park beckoned me, "Sit among our flowers, read Don Quixote and adapt to the news." If I did that, whatever came, I would be ready.

Pooja was there that day. She knelt beside me at my worst five months ago, gripping her hand in a fit of uncontrollable tears. That was the night before my first escape.

The sun will come out in the afternoon, I repeated. *Watch a movie. Let the thoughts stay for later. Time for Peter to play.*

The man from Emanuel Medical Center called again, "The blood culture was positive," but he did not say what grew. He mumbled "candida" then changed his answer to "bacteria." I found the doctors circled up for morning rounds. I interrupted Amanda Posner by briefing her and handed my phone to her. She walked off with it.

When she returned, she said she went through the same maze of words with the man on the line. A doctor on Infectious Disease Team called Emmanuel and made the person on the other line go into the lab and read the cultures again.

"Not candida," (*the panic was unnecessary…thank God!*) "We'll try to treat through the infection" (*for now, no surgery*).

Candida is yeast. Candida Lusitania was the yeast we all feared, the yeast that would have meant scanning his entire body to find its hiding spot. With Peter's activity levels, now that he no longer used his pacifier, that would be torture to him. "Not candida." We repeated back and forth.

In the afternoon, the beeping from his IV pole, leads and blood pressure cuff wore me down. His tubes twisted with every movement. The beeping persisted in an unusually frequent manner. The break from Peter usually came after lunch. It was time. My lunch tray sat empty on the table.

To our sweet nurse, I exclaimed, "Rather than break this beeping pump, I'm leaving!"

The kids would arrive that night. *Tonight I plan to leave the hospital at 5:30 p.m. If I take only one hour for my break now, rather than two, I can give myself permission to leave this evening, even as he is still awake.*

I carried my book to read in the sunshine. In the afternoon, the clouds still hung over the sky.

Whenever I left his room, I prepared my bag for wherever I might go: security badge, cell phone, notebook, reading book.

Having not read Zélie's letters the day before, I bore the weight of carrying her letters along with Don Quixote. It was unlikely I would read the novel. In that section, Zélie is dying of breast cancer, but praying for a cure.

Sitting on the wooden bench in my park among the flowers I read letters filled with urgency as she sought a pilgrimage and prayed for a miracle. They rode a train to Lourdes. It exhausted her and was full of trouble. No cure came. Zélie continued to hope.

Zélie walked alongside me. I was not dying of breast cancer. I did not have thoughts racing through my mind about how my children need me just a little longer and how since they need me, perhaps God will not take me.

Zélie hoped God would allow her to stay just a little

longer. She did not pray for a complete cure, just a few more years to help her daughter, Leonie, whom she had just learned was abused by a servant in the house. Zélie wanted to rebuild this child's spirit. Nothing for herself; her children were her purpose. Though her lace-making business was a success, her reason to strive was her life with her husband and children.

After reading, I completed my break by walking along the path. My reflections ran the pace of my walk.

God answered our prayers. Yesterday, when Pearl brought the Eucharist to me, she said to thank God for little victories. "We'll take what we can get," she added.

The Broviac would stay in. That meant two fewer surgeries. We could continue to pray. We did not have to pray for great and global things. God could answer those prayers. He could also answer little ones. Maybe not with direct answers. He would help us get through.

With a pause before leaving the garden, I asked, *what did it all mean?* Staring at the flowers, the garden answered, "It is like these, the little things along the way, the prayers answered."

The ups and downs were hard to understand, one minute up, the next minute down.

But maybe it was only hard when we expected it all to end one day. We drive ourselves mad with the question: when will it be over?

It will never be over.

Accepting that is the first step to sanity.

The next step is finding things that can be joyful. Those are the flowers. And they are vermillion, purple and dandelion. The herbal fragrance filled the path.

The sun came out as I read. The garden's gift to me.

Chapter 10

The Transfiguration

Peter and his companions had been overcome by sleep, but becoming fully awake, they saw his glory and the two men standing with him. (Luke 9:32)

He hardly knew what to say, they were so terrified. Then a cloud came, casting a shadow over them; then from the cloud came a voice, "This is my beloved Son. Listen to him." (Mark 9: 7-8)

My morning, mothering rhythm returned to me after my children and husband arrived. The children's clothes lay on the chair so I could stealthily dress them one at a time when they arose from sleep, then usher them to the playroom where, hopefully, the televisions were off. Regular visits occurred Saturday through Monday. It was never long enough. Some moments on Sunday felt never short enough. The hospitalizations and separation atrophied my patience.

Every visit was worth it.

In the breadth of that visit, I could not bear to tell the children they would leave a day earlier, Sunday instead of Monday. My imagination painted the sadness filling their faces.

They never wanted to leave.

The hospital was their place with unlimited playroom toys and nurses delighted by their conversational skills. Family House was theirs with new beds, pictures and toy-filled living rooms. At every departure, Miriam hurt the most. The sight of her pain broke my heart.

Tomorrow would be Monday, Labor Day, September 5. As a child, my family and I camped on Labor Day at Burney

Falls. My husband, children and I never did much for this holiday. Instead of riding my bike through California Redwoods, I would be alone. The Family House bulletin board announced an afternoon BBQ. *A hotdog sounds good.*

To renew the hope I felt seeing the ocean with Brian, I petitioned Kyle for a visit to the beach. The sand, surf and scenes enraptured the children. We soaked in their joy, albeit with a little heartache. It was no family trip without Peter. Our little family was incomplete.

The waves frightened Regina. She remained firmly planted on my lap. The sun warmed my skin as the wind nipped away. How good to bask in the elements after the sanitary conditions of the hospital.

We hiked from the beach up the hill to the Sutro Baths. As a single woman on an adventure, my former boss, Cathy took my friends and me to this restaurant. A year later, Kyle and I found it without a map when I was pregnant with James. How satisfying to return again.

After waiting forty minutes for a table on a crowded Sunday afternoon, the $2 cups of milk and overpriced clam chowder disappointed. Following the meal, we trekked down the sun-scorched path to the car. A man whipped a kite around the sky like a ribbon dancer. We stood captivated while the pigeons played the Pied Piper with James.

In the evening, my heart filled my chest. It felt tender under the pain of how right everything was. From that bistro table, I watched Kyle sear steak and eggs for me in the Family House kitchen. My mind wandered. The forest of my many reflections surrounded me.

Everyone has their cross. Perhaps God gave us grace in our marriage that we might be able to face what the outside world threw us. We take what comes; embrace the chaos;

wish we had worn sunscreen and cope with life when the good things are gone.

On the heels of their departure, the emptiness crept in. The color drained from the world until nothing was left but black-and-white. Walking was the only help.

To walk
    and walk
        and walk
        until the emotions
        and the emptiness fade into the distance,
    the scenery begins to pigment with color
    and after long enough,
my feet hurt and I am eager to get back to sit down and rest.
I finish the day as I started, moving forward.

Langston Hughes' "Mother to Son"[1]

Well, son, I'll tell you:
Life for me ain't been no crystal stair.
It's had tacks in it,
And splinters,
And boards torn up,
And places with no carpet on the floor —
Bare.
But all the time
I'se been a-climbin' on,

---

[1] "Mother to Son" (1922) Wikipedia, located online at https://en.wikipedia.org/wiki/Mother_to_Son. The poem was originally published in 1922 and is in the public domain.

And reachin' landin's,
And turnin' corners,
And sometimes goin' in the dark
Where there ain't been no light.
So boy, don't you turn back.
Don't you set down on the steps
'Cause you finds it's kinder hard.
Don't you fall now —
For I'se still goin', honey,
I'se still climbin',
And life for me ain't been no crystal stair.

Dark days happen.

It was too dark. Looking for hope, I found none. I looked for hope for a normal life, for freedom from hospital visits, for a home with my children altogether, where my eight-month-old son is stimulated by his siblings and not by hospital pumps. Where freedom meant being in a field of wildflowers rather than simply walking with my son outside the unit. Where he no longer squints outside in the shade on recycled rubber but on the beach.

There marked the change. No longer could I remember what it was like to be home.

In the first 24-hours after saying goodbye to my family, the emptiness grew and the darkness filled my sight.

Of course, we would go home eventually. Of course, life would not always be like this.

In the moment, it hurt that life was like this.

It hurt that the greatest moment of hope today occurred when doctors from the Immunology Department suggested if they find something amiss with his immune system a medication might boost it.

We cannot turn back.

What other choice would there be? It would be this or it would not be Peter.

He looked so complete. He smiled at me before I left the hospital that day.

"Don't you fall now —"

"It's kinder hard…"

"Don't you fall now —"

Where were our landings or corners? How I hoped to God a corner would come soon.

Tuesday morning awoke to the morning light. Things were brighter in the morning.

With time and acceptance, I gained my strength back after every family visit. Then I moved forward. They are the "gone days," the "dark days." They happen. No one can be strong all the time.

The sun appeared today. I rested, read, and decided if we must stay, Kyle and I would trade places on the weekend.

None of this made the darkness go away. It went away with tears and the morning, allowing that part of me to breathe, accepting it. The dark thoughts did not overpower me. Regardless, it was okay to acknowledge they were there.

Peter improved. He became an awake, alert, playful, perfectly predictable, sitting-up infant.

What did it take to be at peace? Very little. Peace has no requirements or special circumstances. Though I found that some things help.

I could lose everything. God is all that is left. *There must be a way to make that enough.* He did not mean for us to literally hate the things or people in life, but to survive when they are absent. It would not feel good, but I could live through it.

Adapt or die, my two choices. I was not alone. Those words possessed the power to move me through another day.

Chapter 11

Coming Down the Mountain

Suddenly, looking around, they no longer saw anyone but Jesus alone with them

As they were coming down from the mountain, he charged them not to relate what they had seen to anyone, except when the Son of Man had risen from the dead. So they kept the matter to themselves, questioning what rising from the dead meant. (Mark 9: 8-10)

The SPINT2 mutation is an autosomal recessive mutation. It is, perhaps, a 1 in 50,000 chance that Kyle and I should both possess it. Yet we do. While our children had a 25% risk of inheriting it from both of us, only Peter did. That Kyle and I should find each other was statistically unlikely. Yet here we are. For the first time, the understanding seeped into my mind that there was a high-risk of mortality. Each of the three studies said so.

In the beginning, I planted myself by the window afraid to articulate what was present in my mind. I knew what was happening.

Other infants died.

But not Peter; no, my Peter did not die. He was saved.

Because of his cleft, we were already connected to UCSF. Only one other SPINT2 patient had a cleft lip/palate.

The doctors revealed this information to us as we met around a weighty conference table, surrounded by whiteboards whose markings Dr. Henry vigorously erased. A handful of physicians, a case manager, Kyle and I sat in overly large and supremely comfortable spinning chairs. Instead of a great debate over the loss of sodium, we learned we are mutants. They called this a "family meeting." In the last meeting, in the same room with Dr. Li, we made an advance directive. This was different, Dr. Henry explained.

They interpreted my clouded expression as my concern over the ethics of a study they proposed from Toronto. A biopsied piece of Peter's intestine would be cloned, grown in a lab in Toronto into an "organoid," a miniature organ in vitro. We called it "little Peter."

My mind was elsewhere.

The child in my womb might have Peter's same condition. There was a 25% chance we would do this again. There was a 25% chance we would have two children with these needs and hospital stays.

25% filled 90% of my vision.

Remember when life was not like this? In the morning, I tidied the room. When I clicked a Facebook link called, "the spiritual practice of decorating a nursery," I recalled preparing baskets for Peter's changing table. At Michaels, I bought six matching pewter baskets on clearance. As I folded the tiny onesies James wore as an infant, I prayed for the baby who was to come. Serenity rather than devastation ruled the moment.

In the park, Summer and I discussed "imperfectly perfect" moments. The moments at home before this admission seemed perfect. She probed, "Even in those beautiful five days at home, did you worry?"

I did.

When I unpacked those onesies a year ago, I probably worried, too.

What was life now?

In those days, every day, I woke in a place that was not mine with people above me, below me and to the sides of me. The kitchen was not mine but shared with several other families. I walked out a door with a front desk, down a public street and into a large hospital. I greeted people I saw every day for one week and then saw only sporadically after their shifts changed. To some nurses, I connected during difficult times. In conversation, my manner was cordial when down, friendly and funny when up. As an extrovert, I loved discussions with the residents and meeting the nerdier department doctors. New people introduced themselves every day. It was a game to recall their names and departments when they walked in the door and learn a new medical word every day.

Whenever my family visited, I snapped at them easily. Emotion inundated my heart on the drive home, part rage, part tears.

After all this, it was Saturday and I was going home... alone.

Peter stayed.

Kyle came to trade places as previously discussed. Father and son could experience much need time without mom in the room distracting son. The month that passed since they lived together was too long for father and son to be apart. Dr. Posner and Dr. Henry encouraged this. Even though I wanted to push through the hospitalization, I knew I needed respite.

It was dark when I arrived home. The children were nestled all snug in their beds, and in a squall, I straightened the house, cleaned, washed, put things away and arranged pillows. Not the tornado I sometimes experienced when over-whelmed at how much there was to do. It was with anger.

Was I resentful towards life? Was I bitter that I was not home to care for it myself? What was happening?

As I progressed through the house my head cleared. Irritable thoughts in bed circled my mind over who at Family House hand-washed dishes and left them on the counter to dry every day.

"You forgot your maid at home...put your dishes away," my imaginary note read.

It was as if all my raw edges were turned inside out.

Studying the edges showed me I experienced a profound lack of freedom. Strangers filled my every day. At home, it rose to the surface.

I cleaned and organized. I made it my own.

The next day, I redecorated. It would be Autumn in August. Why not? The next time Peter would come through the door, the calendar would read "September."

In the nursery, I painted a final topcoat on the custom-mix Deco green dresser for Peter, who would soon be home. The supplies lay out where I left them the day I left.

I created that room. I loved that room.

The wall is coral because I painted it. I hung homemade, deep orange curtains with a modern white floral motif. I dressed that Art Nouveau bed in a loud, Miami-inspired quilt. On the wall, I hung "The Scream," a 1940's mirror, and an art print of the Madonna who played with the fingers of the infant Christ. I designed the wall décor: reclaimed wood, painted in coral, cut into arrowheads, nailed to the drywall above a Louis blue, Annie Sloan chalk painted desk, fixed up from the side of the road. This was my favorite room.

This room was my art. It welcomed me home and filled my cup.

Leave last Saturday alone. It was the hospital and a bundle of anxiety. Friday night was Family House, restless legs, and my body rejecting the mattress. Today is Sunday, and I am home. Only for one more night. Did it matter?

No! It did not!

I had changed.

The worries of life mattered little now. People told me I was strong before, but I never felt it. Now I did.

Still, there were those dark days when I felt ruined and helpless. As time passed, I understood more about the gravity of my son's condition. If those chromosomes had come together any different, he would not have SPINT2, and he would not be Peter. I no longer had to blame myself or search for that moment when I rerouted the course of his development.

"God meant for you to have Peter...and God meant for you to have this baby," Dr. Posner exhorted to me standing beside Peter's hospital crib.

If I stayed open to the challenges before us, rather than cling to the life of security and comfort, and threw myself into the will and wonder of God, he would do amazing things. He would work in me with his power in a way, thrilling, incredible and painful. Like the feeling of trusting a friend or spouse, free and synchronous, but with the added feeling of flying.

And my bed felt good.

Chapter 12

The Institution of the Eucharist

Peace I leave with you; my peace I give to you. Not as the world gives do I give it to you. Do not let your hearts be troubled or afraid. (John 14:27)

Remember the word I spoke to you, 'No slave is greater than his master.' If they persecuted me, they will also persecute you. If they kept my word, they will also keep yours. (John 15:20)

Alongside Kyle at the crib in the hospital, before we traded places again, I remarked on the roundness of Peter's head and mused, "Looks like he's more than hydrated."

Peter's fontanelle was sunken no more. His nurse, Kelly, who with a jolly spirit regularly pronounced Peter's name with an artificial British accent, rubbed his head and eyed him suspiciously. She observed what I noticed yesterday. Only she knew more.

His fontanelle bulged.

Kelly contacted the doctor.

Kyle left for home. I stayed.

The doctor presented herself and, tactfully, explained the possibilities. It could mean there is excess fluid in his skull, bleeding, an infection or something growing in his brain. Furrowing my eyebrows, I attempted to make the information sink in, yet it drained slowly.

Doctors restated possible explanations again and again.

Amy said, "if it happened to us, we would have a pounding headache, but with his open fontanelle, there is room for his brain to go somewhere."

I relayed the information to Kyle by phone.

The doctors raised his antibiotics to meningitis levels. They scheduled a spinal tap. Dr. Vivek Chenoy, the GI fellow, was the best at spinal taps. The team agreed he should do it.

It seemed unbelievable. Peter was still playing. A young, tall, neurologist, who reminded me of a bald Matthew McConaughey, approached Peter and felt his head, examining his face expression. Peter was active, responsive. "I see no signs of sunsetting in his eyes," he said. "Sunsetting" is when the pupils will not move up to the top of the eyes.

"That's reassuring," he added. They interpreted everything I said as reassuring, everything, except that Peter's fontanelle bulged.

Preparing to pray the Liturgy of the Hours, I opened my Breviary to discover it was the feast of the Exaltation of the Cross.

How could I exalt the Cross? There was a great emptiness around me, grasping for relationship. I was alone.

My parents raised me in the Catholic Church, but I was not raised in suffering. Today, in the reading, I see that St. Paul wrote for me, "How could you be so stupid? After beginning in the spirit, are you now to end in the flesh? Have you had such remarkable experiences all to no purpose—if indeed they were to no purpose?"

We are in exile. I am without a home. I am estranged.

Why minimize the suffering? Just say it for what it is.

When I was young, God worked astounding things in my heart. He brought amazing people into my life. He delighted me with his love.

Now, I was not even old. Yet, I shuddered to think that I had many more decades to live. Let it not be like this past year.

God did not draw me out for nothing. He did not woo my heart for naught. Would I have union with God apart from suffering? In all that consolation, it felt like it was possible. Then I married. My spouse was my consolation; my children were my consolation.

Sunday, my reflection highlighted the beauty of my life, my home, my children and my capability. Monday, it was the beauty of my marriage and gladness in my spouse, the reasons I married him. Tuesday, the goodness of the little things; I saw past small disappointments. Tuesday afternoon, the disappointments mounted and weighed heavy on my back. Tuesday evening, I knew something was wrong. *"It will never end,"* I said inside my heart.

"When will it end?" I asked the Lord.

To pray, that was something in itself. "Please God, clear this traffic."

"Please God, make it end."

"Protect our future, Lord."

There was something deeper in my prayers than ever before.

In prayer, I tried to fathom these events and find courage. Our Lady was there at the cross. On this night, seven years ago at 3 a.m., I miscarried. Since then, it always felt this feast day was for me.

Kyle brought the current volume of the Breviary to me. Searching online to find the week in Ordinary Time, I beheld the readings for the day: The Exaltation of the Holy Cross.

Christ showed us the way.

This life is a mystery to me. I will keep trying.

During our 7:30 p.m. chat, Kyle did not recognize the title *1984* when I considered I might watch the movie. Our pride in cultural knowledge exaggerated my aghast reaction.

Tori's favorite book is *1984*. I quickly relayed our silly conversation to her. We laugh heartily at numbers, at the confusion, at everything we could think of that has to do with nothing. With deep-throated belly laughs that caused me to cough, I felt physical relief from the pain of the mattress, Family House and Peter's admission.

God gave solace. What more can I say? If there was consolation, I should not run from contemplating the cross because of hopelessness.

The next morning, following the procedure, Vivek came to the room in scrubs. Peter was sleepy from the anesthesia. A small mark remained on his lower back. "Everything went well." There was nothing remarkable.

Under sedation, radiology conducted an MRI. Unremarkable. His brain was normal. His heart, lungs, and brain are normal. I think of the cool dad I met at the old Family House, baby Jude and his beautiful mother. Baby Jude was born with a heart condition. The father had not heard of St. Jude, patron and hope in impossible causes.

After another day of anxiety, Peter's fontanelle returned to normal. We never knew why it happened.

Over time, prayer became part of my routine. During my 7 a.m. walk to the hospital, I prayed the rosary. When it finished, I wished there was more. It eased my heart to think of Jesus' sufferings and ours. Those days I reflected on Peter and studies on the SPINT2 mutation. "High risk of mortality..." every study said.

Then, the understanding broke through. Until that moment, in all I did, I was passive, doing what they told me to do to take care of him. For the first time, I perceived how dangerous it all was. Peter was alive because of me. It was true! I was his primary caregiver. Every time we flushed his line with saline or used that alcohol wipe on his Broviac cap or hooked up his TPN, we were keeping him *alive*.

It was not a portal of death, but of life.

It was not the case that when something went wrong that I failed. He might have been dead, but for the things I did. In the largest study with 22 kids, 12 died.

Dr. Posner and I talked about the causes of death (electrolyte imbalance and complications from TPN, meaning infections). We talked about what they meant when they referenced poor quality of life (frequent hospitalizations).

He survived infections. We survived frequent hospitalizations. We can handle this!

Peter would not be alone. His life will not stop because of this. We chose early on to homeschool our children. The work could come with us. Peter has sisters and a brother. Friends from parallel play can forget each other, but Peter is part of a family. This family is strong and good. He has wonderful doctors who love him. This is a teaching/research hospital. If any new research or experimental treatments develop, UCSF will be on the cutting edge.

Nothing I did was useless when done with love. It is the Little Way. That is what I will work on: thinking of it in this manner, pondering these thoughts, considering that this could be part of God's plan. We do not know what that plan will be. How shocking to return to "meant to be" style thoughts.

Before I miscarried our first child, everything seemed providential. After the miscarriage, it all seemed chaos from the Fall. That was my first experience of suffering. Family stability and faith largely preserved me from suffering before then.

At this point, I emailed Camille daily. When I revealed I was pregnant, she replied that she thanked God. Had we known then what we know now, we would have worked much harder to avoid a pregnancy.

God meant for you to have this child...

The future is unclear. Today, I felt hope. These things might not get better, but Christ and I could journey through them together, no matter what comes.

The feeling of my walk Tuesday night was familiar. It happened each time the night before discharge.

Is it real? I asked.

When I walked into Family House I shared the news, "We might go home tomorrow."

The day I have waited for will come tomorrow. *Can it be possible?* Preparations made, prescriptions and supplies ordered. We learned it was better to have Coram's Sacramento office ship to home than wait for the Hayward office to deliver to the hospital. The latter forced us to wait before we could leave. With a deep breath, I think those words, *we are leaving.*

I held my breath for too long.

Can it be? After weeks of waiting, hope was a fearful thing. I prepared myself that something would happen overnight to prevent our leaving. Discharge is always planned, never certain.

He must stay hydrated tonight and not vomit. They increased the TPN. We agreed to mix more breast milk with the formula.

Then there was the ethanol lock. A little alcohol infused at the end of his central line catheter to protect him from those things that find their way into his blood. Could this mean the end of these long admissions?

In the beginning, the likelihood of infection was not great...possible, but more likely to be a normal fever that all kids get. Yet my children were not sick once all summer, only Peter.

Soon infections seemed likely for him. This was his third. One positive blood culture meant two weeks in the hospital. This week closed on five weeks. This admission length matched the "big hospitalization" of his early days, five weeks without interruption. In the middle of this, we had six days at home...six perfect, albeit too short, days.

What would autumn bring us? How many holidays would we spend here? Would Peter turn a corner and have more time home than hospital?

I counted the weeks. By eight months of age, he spent four of those months inpatient. One day, it would change.

Reaching out, I considered grasping at the hope that lay before us. It was a fearful hope. Rationality urged me to accept this as part of life. Fearful acceptance meant not hoping to be home or dreaming of being home an entire month or dreaming of being a family again. How I would love to be together again.

Kyle and I were meant for each other. We need each other. This is the romantic-style marriage, one of the four types Judith Wallerstein wrote about in *The Good Marriage*. It is defined by a sense of destiny. It was written in the stars. Though I never rationally believed marriage must be destiny to be successful, I would be lying if I said I did not think God planned for us to be together since the beginning.

Therefore, we must be together...and detached. That was the lesson. Those were the welcoming words of Fr.

Raphael of Tanzania, our hospital chaplain and friend, as I chatted in the hallway of the PICU. "If anyone comes to me and does not hate his own father and mother and wife and children and brothers and sisters, yes, and even his own life, he cannot be my disciple" (Luke 14:26).

"But not hate," I responded with a smile, "you can love it…just be detached." He burst out laughing and granted me my point. He experienced his own desert away from home.

Detachment. The first spiritual book I ever read was *Abandonment to Divine Providence*. My early days were spent reading the Carmelites, Therese and her night of nothingness, John of the Cross' *Dark Night of the Soul*. How lofty and romantic it seemed then. I understood little of it. How could it be otherwise? Suffering was remote.

God protected St. Therese. She felt he protected some souls in a special way, bringing them up close to him because they would not be robust enough to endure the path otherwise. Still, she suffered. We all must come to it eventually. We all must face the Cross. Then he makes us strong.

What is the Cross and what is hope? There was a danger of superstition: that if I pray in this way, Peter will not go back to the hospital. It must be trust. It must be personal. It has to contain some notion of Heaven as our home. With such a home and family, I could love this world so much I would not want to lose it. I thought that when I held my firstborn.

We are on a journey. Keep it in mind; I held the thought. The excitement for tomorrow grew. I was pregnant, but I pushed the thought of that aside.

Family Photographs

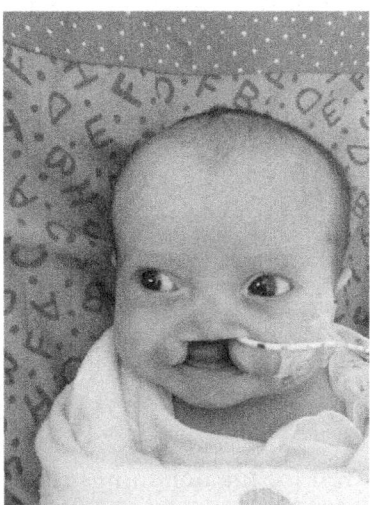

Peter home briefly after
his first hospital admission, March 2016.

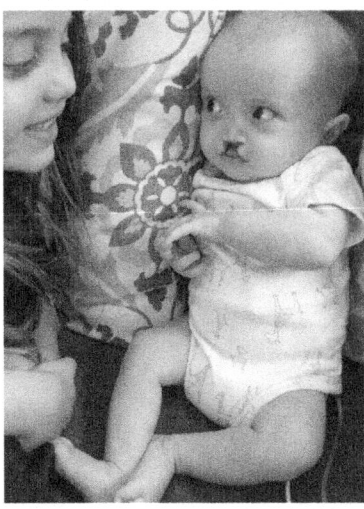

Peter with Miriam at home, May 2016.

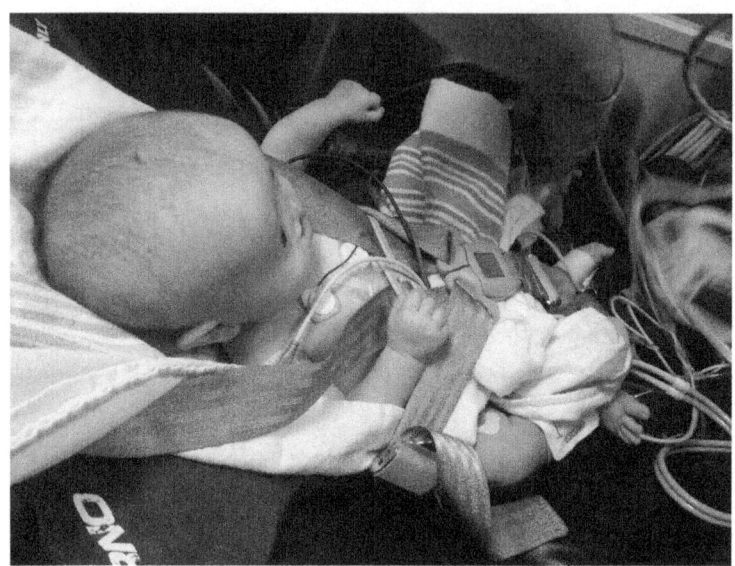

Peter prepared for his helicopter ride, June 2016.

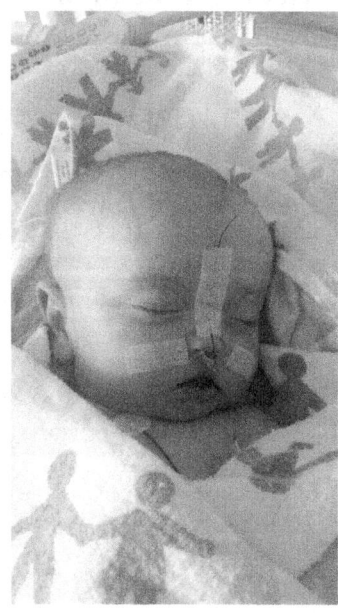

Peter after his cleft lip repair, August 2016.

At the Benioff Children's Hospital, Transitional Care Unit.

Regina and Peter, September 2017.

**The Casey Family: Kyle and Kathryn, Miriam, James,
Regina and Peter Casey,
December 2016.**

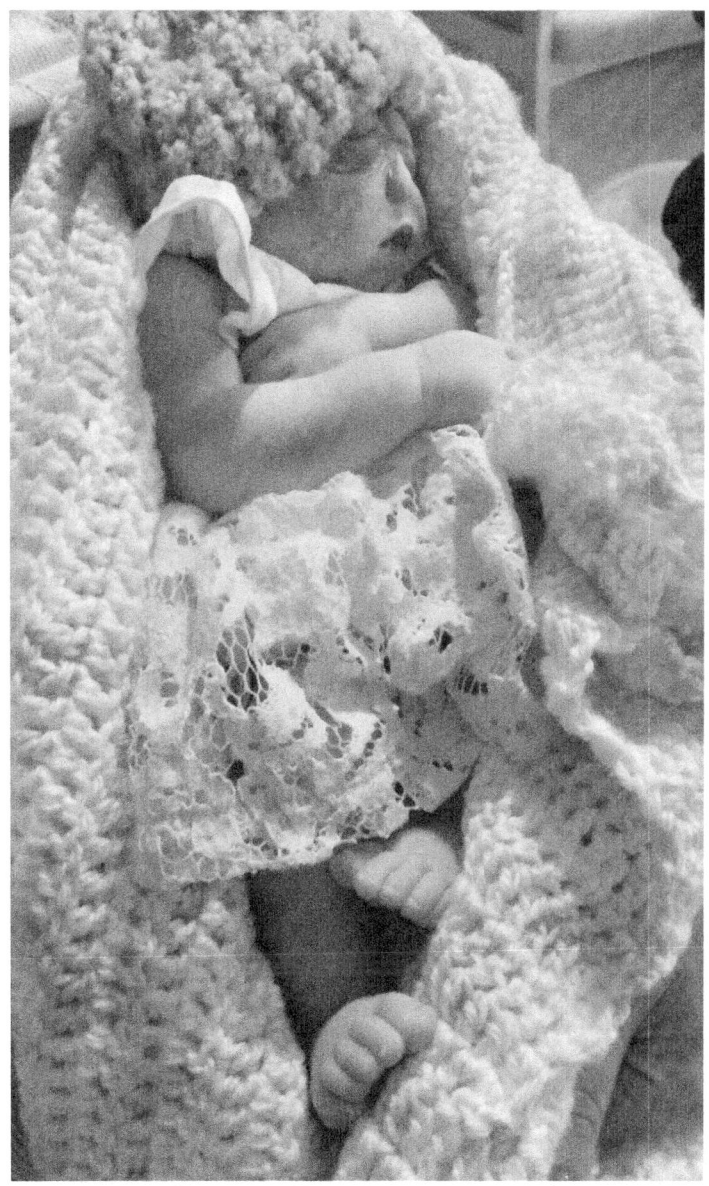

Celeste Casey, March 2, 2017.

**At the funeral home, the night before
Celeste was buried, March 9, 2017.**

**Kathryn at St. Stanislaus Catholic Cemetery
before Celeste's burial.**

**Outside the UCSF
Mission Bay Clinic Building, August 2, 2018.**

Part III

The Sorrowful Mysteries

Chapter 13

The Agony in the Garden

He advanced a little and fell to the ground and prayed that if it were possible the hour might pass by him; he said, "Abba, Father, all things are possible to you. Take this cup away from me, but not what I will but what you will." (Mark 14:35-36)

We did go home. We nearly did, after one more night. One more night was nothing to them. To me, it was everything.

Thursday, we left the hospital for home. The pace of home was akin to being pelted by waves compared to the wading pools of the hospital. The hospital was quiet and methodical, ordered by routines of where to put a dirty diaper and how to order dinner. The schedule was my anchor. The order created a rhythm for the day, rather than an endless series of nothing.

At home, I went from being afraid for his life to seeing him run down the hallway, squealing at his siblings' antics; from his being watched by brilliant medical professionals to being the primary eyes on him; from the loneliness of wandering and sleeping in a city by myself to togetherness, the reunion of a broken family; from a bubble of personal space to the strong shoulder of my husband, and the cuddles of my children; from meditative silence to the screams and whines of multiple kids; from isolation, with only email to connect with friends, to seeing and being in real life; from a daily routine of reading, writing and learning, to endless interruptions; from a terrible mattress as bouncy as the floor to the greatest mattress in the world, those Pima cotton sheets and an artistically fluffed bedspread.

Basically, I went from one sacrifice to another, from loneliness to fear, from contemplation to the busy life of a housewife parenting four kids. Still, I would rather be home.

Home demanded I re-learn how to speak to my spouse and children. We must learn how to live together again. Each return began with collecting data. In my absence, I lost track of current practices, the childish reactions and whims. As the emotional intelligence operative, my job was to notice the patterns in behavior, report and give my professional motherly opinion on the best course of action to Kyle. But I was off-duty for too long.

I bobbed above and below the surface of the water, flailing my arms frantically in a panic. Instead of crying to myself, I exploded. My anger was allowed here. At home, I question God and ask, "why?"

When the surgeons repaired Peter's lip last month, he rejected his bottle for four days. For a few days, he chewed the Pigeon nipple as well as he ever did. One afternoon, he swallowed, he vomited, and he stopped eating for good. Would it never end?

At Peter's follow-up appointment I sat with Amy Chang in the exam room. My phone rang from the hollows of the Petunia Pickle weekender bag. It was Kyle. In the spirit of killing time waiting for Dr. Rhee to approve of Dr. Posner's plans, I answered the phone.

He broke his foot.

Kyle and my dad were on their way to the Emergency Dept. *How was he even able to talk?* I failed to appreciate the gravity of what this would mean. My mind made plans laying out how I could drive him to work with kids in tow. I sought understanding, "Is it your right foot?" No, it was Kyle's left. He could still drive, still work.

When I filled Amy in, she retorted jovially, "Text him to elevate his foot. He can put it on your dad's shoulder."

Amused by the image, I obeyed. Amy and I continued joking until Dr. Rhee returned.

Back home, I did my best to add cooking to my tasks and cover for Kyle, while he lay on the couch with his foot elevated.

"Elevate your foot," his mother wrote more than once by text message.

Kyle had been climbing up and down the ladder in the garage. He stepped down wrong and broke his foot. "It can happen just like that…weird accidents," Aunt Corrine said, who broke the same bone. It could heal quickly, she encouraged.

We found ourselves in new territory. At the onset of our marriage, Kyle and I fell into an egalitarian approach to the division of labor within our home. Each did chores relative to the amount of time spent at home and according to his ability.

Kitchen and cooking stressed me out. He cooked and I cleaned; I managed the children. When new babies came, Kyle presided over the other children's cleanliness, nutrition and behavioral management, while I tended baby. Though Peter passed from the newborn stage, with his medical needs, we maintained the newborn division status.

Now I attempted to cover it all: Peter's needs, the other three kids' needs, Kyle's needs, meals, house, leaving aside my own needs, pregnant though I was.

I ran ragged for two days before falling apart.

The next day, Kyle propelled himself with his right foot on an office chair around the kitchen while he made pancakes.

Grim-faced I pressed ahead, ignoring the exhaustion of my pregnancy. It pained Kyle to see me suffer. He despised his uselessness.

Regina kept me at arms' length, no longer my cuddle bug. Her eyes betrayed her guardedness since my absence. We would have to build that back gradually.

James' sensitivity increased his whining and wailing. Miriam clung to the scraps of time I threw her, eager for her siblings to disappear that she might have me for herself. My body competed with them all, demanding rest. My life dictated activity.

Where was my guardian angel now? What happened to the silence, the prayer and the self-care? In San Francisco, I knew how to take care of myself where there was nothing to think about other than how to care for myself. Prayer, exercise, writing, art and friendship buoyed me up, along with a little shopping.

But now?

Prayer? My mind flitted from thing to thing here at home. Interior quiet seemed elusive. A one-mile bike ride to the adoration chapel would achieve physical and spiritual wellness. But I was so tired. The need to be home held me back. My escapes consisted of weekly labs, drawn by me, delivered to and processed by Quest, weekly weight checks with Dr. Li, weekly bank runs and Sunday mass. There were already too many reasons to leave.

Exercise? But the tiredness...if I could recover from the tiredness, then perhaps I would have exercised.

Writing? Daily. The weekly newspaper column, the YLI[1] Newsletter, the blog posts, the emails, the journal, the spiritual writing implemented that desire. No shortage of opportunities existed.

Art? In my home, I realized the urge to create. Macramé and watercolor in the hospital were mere substitutions to fill the void of my first artistic love: design.

Friendship? A phone call or text made it happen. We were in the same county, now. I could see them *in vivo*, in real life.

Would I run in circles or actually grow this time? The same struggles appeared: to pray, to think of God, to be calm, to be at peace.

The house cannot be cleaned in one day. I can scrub one room at a time. Let me start with family and learning to live together. Let me see my friends.

Yes, I much desired to see my friends.

When I wrote about life, hope lifted me from hovering so close to despair. If I dared leave the words behind, every attempt to stand led to a crash.

I telephoned Fr. Bill for help.

He asked for an update: pregnancy, Peter's infection, near-miscarriage, infection, surgery, bulging fontanelle, Kyle's foot...what else?

Fr. Bill's voice called to mind the liturgy of my childhood and adolescence. The man who held the crucifix high above his head as he processed on Good Friday, chanting, "Behold, behold/the wood of the cross/on which is hung our salvation/O come, let us adore him." His voice was the

---

[1] Young Ladies Institute, a national Catholic women's organization

2222

voice of reassurance and fatherly affection. In his tone, I heard the shrug in his shoulders, the bewilderment in his spirit. He wanted to help, to take it away, but all he could offer was this, "I don't know why this is happening, but this is a dark night...and you just have to hold on for dear life."

Fr. Bill recommended I read *Come be my Light*, a book of Mother Teresa's letters to her director revealing her interior desert. It waited up high with the other books on spirituality in the office. Because he suggested it, I would pick it up again.

We do not know why this is happening. That was the first time those words stood their ground as an answer to the question, "why?"

For the first time, it was okay to answer, "I do not know."

For the first time, it was okay not to know.

The future frightened me. I chose to face the trial that lay before me and ahead of me. A few days later, I might crumble inside, but for now, I managed to stand. With determination, I prepared to keep moving forward, to live life. September disappeared and October began.

Chapter 14

The Scourging at the Pillar

When he was about to die under the blows, he groaned, saying: "The Lord in his holy knowledge knows full well that, although I could have escaped death, I am not only enduring terrible pain in my body from this scourging, but also suffering it with joy in my soul because of my devotion to him.". (2 Maccabees 6:30-31)

Five days later, I returned to the OB for my 20-week ultrasound on October 10. Kelsey, the nurse practitioner wanted to make sure there were no pockets of blood that could have caused the spotting weeks ago.

In the same room where we discovered Peter's cleft, my belly slathered in warm gel, the technician did her job. She took her photos. I searched for thoughts to pass the time. They filled with hopes for a girl...and nursing...and no SPINT2.

Rather than leave Peter and his complexity with a babysitter, Kyle stayed with the children. Despite our experiences, this was routine. The technician took her snapshots and measurements. After a pause, she printed, ripped the photos from the printer and stood up.

"I thought you would let me see—" I started.

"I just need to show these to the doctor." She tossed a towel to me and hurried out of the room. The last image of the baby remained on the screen. Sitting up, I studied it. Something was different.

My eyes darted back and forth between the screen and the poster of an ultrasound baby on the wall. On the poster, the baby's head appeared so much rounder. My baby's head looked flat by comparison. An unfamiliar, older doctor rushed in and spoke. As he caught his breath, he said many words. Out of the cloud, I heard, "It looks like anencephaly." After more words, he added, "It's bad."

The fog settled over my mind. The technician returned. Peering through the curtain, I requested a photograph. She gave me one less clear than what I had seen. "Maybe it's weird to ask now, but what sex is…"

"It looks like a girl," she murmured.

We had hoped for a girl.

They ushered me into another room where Kelsey talked to me. My face was still as I listened. It looked like there was no brain. There might be some; they could not tell. They would refer out. Her words were definite and vague all at once. The grip of the grit it took to face everything with Peter held me in one piece. With the same steady voice of morning rounds, I looked her in the eyes and asked, "Is it fatal?"

She replied, "Yes."

My head nodded. Whatever else passed was left in the fog. Standing up, hazily I walked out and called Kyle above the stairwell. There are a million ways to tell your spouse and father of your child his baby will die. As I walked down the stairs, he listened to what I saw and what they said. In the parking lot, I ended the conversation, "I am on my way home now," and we hung up.

In the van, I sent a text message to Erin, Joanna, Mallory, Tori and Lauren before I started to drive, "The baby has anencephaly. She does not have a brain."

The phone quickly pinged, "Oh my gosh, I am crying for you right now. I am so sorry."

Through the tears down Briggsmore Ave, I cried out, "Damn it! Damn it! Damn it!" *Why God?*

My mother was in the living room when I opened the front door and walked inside, placing my things on the entryway table. She looked at me expectantly waiting to hear the sex of the baby. There were a million ways I could have told her. "There is something wrong with the baby's head."

She looked at the picture briefly when I pointed to the flat spot. Kyle and I walked down the dark hallway to our bedroom and shut the door. "I don't think we should wait to tell the kids," was my only constructive thought.

Zélie prayed, "Lord, grant me the grace that this child may be consecrated to you, and that nothing may tarnish the purity of its soul. If ever it would be lost, I prefer that you should take it without delay."[1]

Five more days passed. The Emergency Dept. doctors admitted Peter to the hospital on October 15.

We cannot know why this is happening.

This was a dark night. It was not the night of poetry. This was the night of real life.

Thoughts tempted me to ruminate. When the thoughts doubted, "God why are you doing this?" my will countered, "We do not know why this is happening."

That answer helped.

How could I deliver three perfectly healthy children, and then Peter, who will have many, many problems? We do not know.

Why the timing of all these things?

Why did Kyle break his foot?

---

[1] Celine Martin, *The Mother of the Little Flower (1823-1894)*, Trans: Fr. Michael Collins, S.M.A. (Charlotte, North Carolina: TAN Books and Publishers, 2005).

Was there some cosmic book written, dictating these things under the heading, "it was meant to be," or is it just chance, the chaos of a fallen world? Did Kyle just step off the ladder wrong?

We cannot know. There were timeless truths I knew: God permits things to happen; God works all things for good for those who love him; God is love. Somehow those truths have to square with the situation at hand.

I married my husband because I saw he loved me the way God loved me. Our marriage taught me how to love God through this crisis by the example of my love for my husband. "We are on the same side," cooled the heat during a fight. It was not me against Kyle.

It was not me against God.

God wants good things for us. He knows better how to bring it about.

If I started there, then my eyes opened to all the ways God helped us. The confluence of events made things easier, not harder. Family House loaned us a family pass for the Academy of Sciences. Miriam's birthday landed on Monday, Kyle's day off. The whiteboard announced Sharon was Peter's nurse for the day. Mara ended her night shift in tears over Peter's broken Broviac, repaired not fifteen minutes later. A Keurig appeared in our room as a mysterious gift delivered to "Peter Casey." The smell of fresh coffee in the afternoon made me feel so fine. While Kyle's foot throbbed, I drove confidently enough through the city. The list went on. We were not without comfort.

At a different time, such a reading as "the sufferings of this present time are as nothing compared with the glory to be revealed for us" (Rom 8:18), would have elicited a bitter whisper, "That's a tall order."

The bitterness evolved to a dare, "Really? Prove it."

During this latest pilgrimage to UCSF, the God of my youth, the God I knew and trusted, to whom I stayed devoted but felt far from these seven years of marriage, visited me.

Obedient to Fr. Bill, I read *Come Be My Light*. Halfway through, Mother Teresa quoted another saint, "There would come a time when God would fill what he had emptied."[2]

Sitting on the muted blue couch in the hospital room, I faced the window overlooking the park. In the distance, across town, stood the two pillars, the ivory bell towers of St. Ignatius Church. With the light on the horizon, I drew a deep breath to build my courage and hope.

We used to pilgrimage there. With friends, I drove to the city after the morning traffic cleared, made a holy hour at the Carmelites, noon mass at St. Ignatius, then a picnic on the University of San Francisco lawn at the foot of the Lourdes grotto. Then, if the timing was right, we perused books and prayed the Liturgy of the Hours at Ignatius Press. Those pilgrimages, part of my youth and adventure, stayed in my heart when I came to San Francisco.

The patient coordinator from my OB referred us to a clinic in Stockton for a Level II ultrasound. After that, I would be sent to a place like Stanford or UCSF for care. Working it out on the telephone, I scheduled directly with UCSF. That appointment was Thursday.

What would Thursday bring? My friend said maybe they would be wrong. There are many pro-life stories in which

---

[2] Mother Teresa. *Come Be My Light: The Private Writings of the "Saint of Calcutta."* Ed. Brian Kolodiejchuk, M.C. (New York: Doubleday, 2007), 181.

the starring doctor who recommends abortion is totally wrong, and how glad they were they did not abort because their perfect baby is theirs forever.

We would never do anything directly to end this pregnancy, I prepare myself to tell the medical professionals who try to suggest otherwise.

At the wide window, I recalled when we sat with the genetic counselor, my belly big with Peter's presence. She used the word "abortion" in relation to Peter. "Unless you were to consider abortion…" she said. My hands reached around my belly to envelop my child. Kyle choked on the words that we would never consider it. My body surrounds this baby, desperate to protect it…but helpless.

I spent my adolescence sitting in the pew behind Lorena and Erasmo at St. Stanislaus Catholic Church. Their elder daughter was the flower girl for our wedding. After their son, Adriel, died, we visited with his parents. Erasmo's voice filled with rage as he disappeared into his memories of the things doctors said when they tried to convince them to abort their child. Adriel lived five years.

Now we knew.

The memories play in my mind as I stare out the window.

All Dr. Posner can say, from the depth of her 5-foot-1 frame, is "I am so, so sorry."

Does she remember what she said before, "God meant you to have this baby"? I believed those words were from God when she said them. They were still from God now.

It was time for my appointment. Kelly, Peter's nurse, knew.

Kyle walked out with me. We left the hallways of the TCUP, entered the elevator and exited the security gates, took the long walk down the bright corridor to the Gateway Building. In a state of the art room, Dr. Rosenstein commenced the ultrasound. Kyle sat on one side and Dr. Rosenstein on the other as we watched the large television screen on the wall. Quickly her hand came to the point.

Beginning with the baby's feet, she illuminated us step by step on what she saw. Her words guided us around each of the baby's body parts. First the feet, then the legs, moving the wand over my swollen torso we see baby's torso, spine and heart. It beat steadily. Her heart is perfect. The doctor moved the wand steadily up to her neck, her head and then...nothing. She lifted the wand off of me.

Pausing across the chasm of before and after this moment, I threw myself into Kyle's arms and cried, "My baby!" His muscular arms engulfed me as I sobbed.

"How can she be alive?" A wall of shock strained the words.

Gently and scientifically Dr. Rosenstein explained, "A baby does not need their brain to grow inside you. She will not likely die during this pregnancy. I can induce early. I can—"

"We will not terminate the pregnancy," I interrupted. Not those words. No one can say those words to me.

There was nothing else to discuss. With a towel, I scraped the gel off my stomach and stood up. We walked out, rode down the elevator and looked for air outside. After sitting a short period, we agreed to name our baby Celeste. Beyond that, there was nothing to discuss. We returned to Peter.

As we entered the double automatic doors to the Children's Hospital, we encountered Jen, the resident who took care of Peter last year during the worst of it. She had a baby girl in her arms. My eyes fixed on her baby's beautiful completeness. After Peter was born, I stared at other baby's noses, now my eyes admired the rounded cranium.

Distractedly, I gave away, "We just found out our baby has anencephaly."

Before the elevator, we met Dr. Posner in her scrubs. I told her, too. She hugged us. "I don't know what to say. I am just so, so sorry."

Back in our familiar place, I held Peter close.

It made sense what Dr. Rosenstein said. We could induce early. She said anytime, but we would not consider it until after viability. It made rational sense. I thought so. Kyle thought so. Summer was supportive. Why go through the terrible pain of pregnancy and a difficult full-term delivery? Let this pregnancy to be over as soon as possible. Make it go away. Just get it over with.

In response to my email disclosing my thoughts, Camille, fearful of a decision we would regret, sent me a link from the United States Conference of Catholic Bishops.

It states: "The fact that the life of a child suffering from anencephaly will probably be brief cannot excuse directly causing death before 'viability' or gravely endangering the child's life after 'viability' as a result of the complications of prematurity."

What could gravely endanger the child's life more than the fact that she has no brain? My heart felt torn in two at the desire to be rid of this pregnancy and the statement that confronts me, early induction is against the teaching of the church I believe to be founded and led by God. I must follow her teachings, but I felt angry. I emailed Fr. Bill.

He replied quickly including two links in his email. The first was an explanation of the USCCB's statement.[3] The second was a woman's personal story of carrying her anencephalic baby to term. The first explained we must not deprive an infant of the good of the nurturing that takes place in the womb.

How much more sense this made to me! Rather than pretend like complications of prematurity would take her life, instead this showed me that my daughter would experience a positive good by being with me. As much as I desired to hide away from all that lay before us, and pass to the other side, I would not refuse her the one thing I could give her.

This, I could accept.

We made our decision. We would induce at 37 weeks, full-term, but avoiding the worst of pregnancy, the last three weeks.

From Psalm 121:

I lift up my eyes to the mountains; where is my help to come from?
    The LORD will guard you from all evil;
    he will guard your life.
    The LORD will guard your coming and your going,
    both now and forever.

Summer supported the change in my thinking. I could tell Dr. Rosenstein thought it better for us to induce earlier.

---

[3] Moral Principles Concerning Infants with Anencephaly: Observations on the document by Fr. Benedict Ashley, O.P. https://www.ewtn.com/catholicism/library/fr-benedict-ashley--anencephaly-9677

She raised the idea multiple times, but never opined directly. Each professional we spoke to felt it necessary to tell us all our "options." I cut the genetic counselor off, asserting we would never consider terminating. She responded, "I just want you to know your options, in case you go home and change your mind."

You must keep to what you have been taught and know to be true (2 Tim 3:14).

My prayer was that Celeste would die in my arms.

Chapter 15

The Crowning with Thorns

So Jesus came out, wearing the crown of thorns and the purple cloak. And he said to them, "Behold, the man!" (John 19:5)

Many tears filled those evenings. During the cloud-covered, gloomy days, I practiced *hygge*, a Danish concept of happiness through coziness, candles, textiles and books. My prayers became specific.

And God answered specifically.

"Please God, let us be home for Halloween," I prayed.

The kids' Halloween costumes evolved from thrift store goods. A thrifted prom dress transformed into accents for a flower girl gown to create Cinderella's look. Another prom dress skirt became an ethereal skirt for the fairy godmother. An oversized, orange sweater grew into the shell of a pumpkin. A bear sweatshirt made Peter a mouse. His TPN tubing could be his tail. Rather than a prince, Kyle converted to a pirate. He hobbled on a peg leg, the iWalk from Amazon, supporting his knee, keeping the weight off his broken foot. The celebration was sober.

With November 2nd came a fever. The Broviac policy required a 48-hour rule out.

To prepare myself for what Celeste would look like, I requested a 3-D ultrasound while I was at UCSF with Peter. The eyes might be enlarged. We might learn how severe was the loss. Maybe there would still be a brainstem. If a brainstem, maybe she could have some life outside the womb.

Kyle could not come. Summer accompanied me. I wanted to see Celeste's face, but her head was too low. Mostly, we saw only her perfect back, perfect legs and perfect toes. This was for the best. It felt good to joke the way Kyle and I always joked during ultrasounds, ignoring the bigger picture. I had that moment of laughter at what she should be like, even though it would never be.

"Please God, let us have Thanksgiving at home." We practiced our growing number of traditions: a decorated table, Miracle on 34th Street in the afternoon, bourbon gravy, and failed cranberry sauce. The day ended in satisfaction.

Black Friday came, along with another fever, and 48-hour rule out.

Two more rule-outs followed.

Four Sundays before Christmas, Advent began. The fog persisted.

On Facebook, I see a post from "'King Lear' in Advent" in the *Imaginative Conservative* written by Glenn Arbery reflecting on King Lear and the season:

> "Lear kills the man who was hanging her, but nothing can revive his beloved daughter. 'Why should a dog, a horse, a rat have life,' he asks in anguish over her, 'and thou no life at all?' How many parents, how many spouses, have asked the same question?"[1]

We were home for the Cookie Exchange Party and fulfilled our spur of the moment plans to buy a sorry-looking

---

[1] Glenn Arbery, "'King Lear' in Advent" *Imaginative Conservative*, December 10, 2016. https://theimaginative-conservative.org/2016/12/king-lear-advent-shakespeare-glenn-arbery.html

Christmas tree from Tracy Trees. After decorating, I declared, "I never thought it was such a bad little tree."[2]

In the spirit of *hygge*, everywhere the eye might roam I decorated for winter and Christmas around the house. The rain would not let up. I lit candles every evening.

In a rare bit of joy, we laughed around the breakfast table when Kyle's phone rang. Bacon grease on his fingers prevented the screen from registering his swipe. His sister, Quinn, called again. With dry hands, he picked up.

Trevor, Kyle's brother, at 34-years-old, was dead. He died December 20th. The conversation was short. The news sank in. When Kyle began to cry, we stared at him from our chairs. With his fist, he pounded the table. I quickly ushered him into the bedroom so he could feel and express what he needed to in the way he needed to. Memories flooded my thoughts: Trevor filling balloons for birthday parties, word salad letters from prison, his strange but kind emails, how good he felt to hear me praise him, how good it felt to hear him love our children.

As my husband grieved his brother's death, I looked on helplessly. He lay in bed, unable to act. It was the day everyone thought might happen but prayed would never come.

"Please God, let us be home for the 12 days of Christmas. Don't make me leave Kyle, not now."

The night before Christmas, I attended the Christmas program with Lauren at Big Valley Grace. Joyous strains filled the amphitheater church. In the middle, the merrymaking paused to hear the reflective melody sung by a wom-

---

[2] *A Charlie Brown Christmas,* directed by Bill Melendez (Lee Mendelson Film Productions, 1965). https://youtube.com/playlist?list=PLUckGLPqcTsUSgrotgdUIYUD_3li_8cXR

an about the cold, lonely night. It was not without suffering that this child was born.

He was born to die.

No one says these words, but I thought them throughout Advent and on Christmas Eve. Christ was born to die.

If God in his madness can do that, then there must be some sense in what is happening to us.

My child is born to die. She is meant for Heaven.

I wrote her eulogy while she kicked inside me.

The altar at St. Stanislaus was filled with scarlet poinsettias and two lawn orbs dressed to look like ornaments dramatizing a modern greige palette. A moment at the crèche recalled our first Christmas after my first miscarriage. That night, I touched the feet of Jesus, as if I could touch the foot of my unborn child. Now, I touched my belly.

At home, we read, "A Visit from St. Nick." Ignoring the chaos of an ill-planned Christmas Eve gathering, the children and I processed out with the baby Jesus to the crèche on the fireplace mantle. In the morning, the children squealed because they all believe in Santa. For all the stories we tell, in the sight of the evidence, they were amazed it could be true.

On Christmas day, my mother-in-law said she already knew about Celeste. Quinn had informed my brothers-in-law as well. I would rather people knew, to spare me the pain of telling them. I wished I had known they knew.

December 31st is the 7th day of Christmas.

The year began with Peter's birth. On the Eve of the New Year, we said goodbye to Trevor and prayed for a quick journey to Heaven. The year began with a birth and ended with a death: a death of too-young a man.

After the rosary for Trevor, when we said goodbye to him while he lay in that open casket, Kyle's godmother, also named Celeste, got on her knees and kissed my belly in some pro-life gesture. I escaped, leaving Kyle to tell her what will happen to her namesake. It was hard to look at her after that.

At the dawn of the New Year, I thought, maybe this year will be better. "Hopefully we meet under better circumstances," my husband's relatives told me. They are not aware. We will not meet under better circumstances. The next time we meet will be the funeral for my daughter.

At every moment of every day, I carry a child who is alive, who moves and kicks and causes me discomfort and occasional indigestion. When she is born, she will die.

The only thing I knew about the coming year was the coming death. It will not be my brother-in-law we bury, I thought. It will be my daughter. That will be her casket, her flowers, and her eulogy. The readings will be a promise we will see her again. I will be in tears. I will be the mother, spread over the casket, crying, "you were supposed to die after me...you were supposed to grow old." I will be the woman in the fog. I will be the woman barely breathing. They will wait for me to leave before they leave the church.

"Why is everyone hugging Grandma Casey?" Miriam marveled that day.

"When someone dies, no one is sadder than the mother," I taught her.

It was painful but obligatory to reflect at the turn of the New Year. Peter was born. Peter was sick. We were apart. We were together. Peter is better, but Peter will never be free from trouble. That was no longer the trouble for us. The trouble was Job. We were being tested, allowed to have all these things taken from us in order to test our mettle, our faithfulness to God.

We have been faithful. We have been angry, but we have been faithful. We kept it together. Peter is alive, and we kept it together. We could not have accomplished more this year.

The woman who began the last New Year was a stranger to me. I doubt I will recognize the woman who ends the next year: the woman who has buried her baby, the woman who will know such grief, the greatest grief I ever feared.

The 12 Days of Christmas ended on Epiphany. Three days after Epiphany, Peter's thermometer beeped confirming my suspicion. Another fever and another "rule-out" admission. This time, we stayed for Peter's cleft palate repair.

I thought I was prepared, but he was bigger and stronger this time. He wailed in my presence and at the sound of my voice. They suggested I leave the recovery room so he would calm down. "Fix it, mommy," he begged my heart. "Take away my pain."

"Why don't you take a break?" the nurse suggested as I wept.

Peg warned us, "They either do well with the lip repair and struggle with the palate or vice versa." We were wrongly confident.

Dr. Hoffman, looking like Itzhak Perlman, closed the palate in one surgery. In his scrubs and blazer, accompanied by his entourage of residents, fellows and medical scribes, he passed by, checked on and admired his handiwork. When Peter calmed, we returned to his room in the T-CUP. He wore the arm braces they put on little patients after these surgeries so the patients do not touch their mouth. They call them "no-no's." He wore them just once. Beyond that, we avoided them altogether and kept close watch.

Chapter 16

The Way of the Cross

Then he said to all, "If anyone wishes to come after me, he must deny himself and take up his cross daily and follow me. For whoever wishes to save his life will lose it, but whoever loses his life for my sake will save it. (Luke 9:23)

We decided to consecrate our suffering. Suffering is no good on its own. It must be given to God in order to become holy. In the presence of Fr. Raju, Kyle and I offered the following prayer.

A reading from the book of Lamentations 3:17-26.

My soul is deprived of peace, I have forgotten what happiness is;

I tell myself my future is lost, all that I hoped for from the Lord.

The thought of my homeless poverty is wormwood and gall;

Remembering it over and over leaves my soul downcast within me.

But I will call this to mind, as my reason to have hope:

The favors of the Lord are not exhausted, his mercies are not spent;

They are renewed each morning, so great is his faithfulness.

My portion is the Lord, says my soul; therefore will I hope in him.

Good is the Lord to one who waits for him, to the soul that seeks him;

It is good to hope in silence for the saving help of the
  Lord.

Then we prayed a prayer compiled from other prayers:

I will consecrate this trial. It shall not be an ordinary,
profane thing. It shall be set apart for God. It shall be
taken away from the world. It shall be God's. I consecrate it in the name of the Father, the Son and the Holy
Spirit. May it bring about your glory and draw us closer
to you, through the heart of Mary, the Mater Dolorosa.
To Jesus, through Mary.
  O, Blessed Joseph, you gave your last breath in the
loving embrace of Jesus and Mary. When the seal of
death shall close Celeste's life, come with Jesus and Mary
to aid us. Obtain for us this solace for that hour – to die
with her in our arms and Jesus and Mary's holy arms
around us. Jesus, Mary and Joseph, I commend my soul,
living and dying, into your sacred arms. Amen.

Time and focus shifted from Peter to Celeste. Celeste
Casey, meant for Heaven.
  After the question of surgery was raised and put aside,
the doctor permitted Kyle to switch from a peg leg to a hard
sole shoe.
  Rachel, my Minnesota friend whom I met on pilgrimage
when I was 18 and reunited with when I attended college, in
whose wedding I assisted by playing personal attendant,
agreed to make Celeste a dress: a simple dress with light pink
and white and maybe some pale yellow and lace. The pink
and yellow would represent her sisters.

Lorena agreed to make her a hat. We decided to ask the doctors to put the hat on Celeste before we see her. We desired to see her as she was, and not only for what she was missing.

My sister agreed to make a blanket.

Months ago, I asked. Now in January, I ached to hold these belongings of the daughter I will not have for long. Nothing arrived. On the day I wished most to hold them, Lauren presented a gift bag enfolding a little hat she made, in ballet slipper pink and purple, small and soft, for my daughter. There was a brim attached and a tiny hole at the top for some technical knitting reason. It was the first thing I had of hers.

Holding it, I pictured Celeste's little face, big eyes and all. I could see myself cradling her. I did not run from the feelings. It felt good to cling to them. It felt like holding her.

When I held her, I knew, it would not be for long enough. It would never be for long enough. All my life I thought I would suffer to hold her till she was too heavy to hold, to nurse her till she was too old to nurse. I can never share these words with her. She would never grow old enough to hear them.

Though it hurts so much, I would rather grasp this pain than nothing at all. Better to face all the sadness we will feel with her than to never know her at all. I was glad I did not lose her through miscarriage, glad to carry her this far. It was going to be the way it should be. This strange glory...

"The Greek word for this self-emptying is kenosis, it is the surrender of all that we hold most dear, and for Mary, it was the surrender of her dearest. Long before they looked at one another on Golgotha's place of strangest glory, they had been prepared by many little surrenders for this surrender by which all was restored."[1]

The hat was the first of Celeste's possessions.

Soon after, Carrie sent me a silver necklace with Celeste's name engraved on a small silver disk and *The Book of Joy*.

Kyle could baptize Celeste. We could use water from Lourdes. A bottle of Lourdes water filled during the 2005 World Youth Day pilgrimage lay somewhere in the house. How would I find it from twelve years ago? That same day, my college roommate, Mallory, told me her friend, April planned to send me holy water from Lourdes.

It was Ordinary Time, but it felt like Lent.

"At the cross her station keeping. There was nothing else to be done, except to be there. The presence of our helplessness is our gift to the helpless...it takes the listener into the heart of darkness, and there, at the heart of darkness, is hope, because there is Christ..."[2]

There was nothing to do now but prepare. In January, I requested a three-month break from writing my newspaper column. Facing our every day with a spiritual lens, I could no longer write anything secular. The intensity of my youthful faith returned. I knew my king again. It was the only way the

---

[1] Richard John Neuhaus, *Death on a Friday Afternoon: Meditations on the Last Words of Jesus from the Cross*. (New York: Basic Books, 2001), 79.

[2] Richard John Neuhaus, *Death on a Friday Afternoon: Meditations on the Last Words of Jesus from the Cross*. (New York: Basic Books, 2001), 82.

world made sense. San Francisco was no longer vital to spiritual survival.

In between the tears, I invested more at home, more with the kids and tried to check things off my to-do list. As I cried, holding her hat, Peter sat on my lap. The other children surrounded me, encompassing me with their love and concern.

The storm carried me. Everything turned toward Celeste.

Suddenly, I woke from a dream.

In it, there were nuns and doctors and a hospital where I felt safe and calm. The place was blue, the sheets were blue, the walls were blue, the floor was blue. Looking for a place to deliver Celeste, I wandered in. They were trustworthy there.

Waking, I knew it represented UCSF. Peter was safe near UCSF. The presence of nuns was the presence of God and the Church. Fr. Raphael committed to coming to Celeste's birth.

At the edge of my emotions, I hung close to the cliff, ready to jump or cling to the side, and prayed it would all be over soon. At each sign of grief, I lost control: good grief, grief from living with children, from noise, from them not understanding how to pull their pants up or put on their shoes.

Fresh tears came. Celeste would not experience the church, but she would meet God. "She will encounter God directly. That is enough," I insisted. Maybe what bothered me is that I would not be the one to introduce her to the things I have lived and loved.

My dream felt safe. It was tranquil, untroubled. Neither peaceful nor joyful, just calm. No rage, fear or grief, just a simple resignation, nuns and familiar doctors tending to me in a place I was glad to find.

How would it feel to hold her, to have my arms full? That would make everything all right. It would feel complete.

Then my arms would be empty. *How can I say goodbye?* I have not been able to say hello.

Anticipation consumed me. Giving and functioning were beyond my reach. I wanted to keep walking, but each step led to a dead end. "Stop and stay a while," Richard John Neuhaus encourages the reader in that book, *Death on a Friday Afternoon.*[3]

It was all I could do. There was nowhere else to look because everywhere I looked, there she was.

C.S. Lewis writes in *The Problem of Pain,* "If a mother is mourning not for what she has lost but for what her dead child has lost, it is a comfort to believe that the child has not lost the end for which it was created. And it is a comfort to believe that she herself, in losing her chief or only natural happiness, has not lost a greater thing, that she may still hope to 'glorify God and enjoy Him forever.' A comfort to the God-aimed, eternal spirit within her. But not to her motherhood. The specifically maternal happiness must be written off. Never, in any place or time, will she have her son on her knees, or bathe him, or tell him a story, or plan for his future, or see her grandchild."[4]

---

[3] Richard John Neuhaus, *Death on a Friday Afternoon: Meditations on the Last Words of Jesus from the Cross.* (New York: Basic Books, 2001), 2.

[4] C.S. Lewis, *The Problem of Pain.* (New York: Macmillan Publishing, 1962).

To cope I focused on the birth plan, the childcare plan, the hospital plan, the Peter plan and the Peter emergency plan.

The focus was palliative care, that is, comfort care. At a team meeting in the Fetal Treatment Center, Kyle and I stated we did not want to fight what would happen. Better not risk my body and recovery when death for her was inevitable. Once she was born, they would place her on my chest for skin-to-skin contact. The doctor commended the idea as something that could help with pain management and regulate her breathing. Then Kyle would baptize her. Fr. Raphael would be on call.

To my mother, I emailed the "March 2nd Schedule Based on Maternal Experience of What is Best for the Casey Offspring."

Time	Task
7 a.m.:	Wake-up, dress, breakfast, pack crowd-pleasing lunches such as PB&J
9 a.m.:	Walk to hospital, visit the mother (unless in active labor, text first), third-floor birth center, middle entrance (Betty Irene Hospital)
10 a.m. to noon:	Playroom for the three younger, schoolroom for Miriam
Noon:	Take Regina to family house for a nap, eat with others at Mariposa Park across from the hospital

Play for 30 minutes following lunch

Visit the mother
Return to hospital with Regina following nap

2 p.m. to 4 p.m.:   Playroom for all kids

Early dinner at Peasant Pies

5:30 p.m.:   Return to Family House, dress for
                       bed, tidy room, play in the living
                       room as time permits

7 p.m.:   Bedtime for the three younger
7:30 p.m.:   Bedtime for Miriam

There is nothing more to be done.

Chapter 17

Crucifixion

From noon onward, darkness came over the whole land until three in the afternoon. And about three o'clock Jesus cried out in a loud voice, "Eli, Eli, lema sabachthani?" which means, "My God, my God, why have you forsaken me?" (Matthew 27:45-46)

After this, aware that everything was now finished, in order that the scripture might be fulfilled, Jesus said, "I thirst." There was a vessel filled with common wine. So they put a sponge soaked in wine on a sprig of hyssop and put it up to his mouth. When Jesus had taken the wine, he said, "It is finished." And bowing his head, he handed over the spirit. (John 19: 28-29)

March 1st was Ash Wednesday, exactly 37 weeks gestation. I did not attend mass. Instead, I wandered our hallway slowly packing our suitcases surrounded by my children. In the afternoon, we drove to San Francisco.

Kyle and I arrived at 7 p.m., one hour ahead of schedule. When I am anxious, I over-prepare, then show up early. As we approached the building, entered the elevator and found the third floor, my steps slowed and halted. The fear to approach this thing we prepared for grew. Forty minutes passed in the waiting room. My mind slowed and wandered, settling my nerves.

When we entered, the room reminded me of any other labor and delivery room. I spied the warmer. She would not live long enough to use that.

The nurse left us alone to get comfortable. After discussion with Zoey Julian, the young, African-American chief resident with short hair and a jacket that read "Julian," we determined a Foley bulb would be the best method for dilating my cervix (currently one-centimeter dilated). The other method risked distressing the infant. I wanted every chance of her being born alive, drawing the line of sacrifice just before the option of a C-section. The nurse inserted the balloon. The waiting began.

When it was time, sleep came easily. After a few hours, my shoulders and hips hurt from the hard bed. The Foley bulb was uncomfortable. The nurse checked at 11 p.m. No progress. No contractions. No cramping. Sleeping was elusive after that. Doubts intruded. *I was too early. This is not how it should be. We should have waited. Why were we inducing?*

Zoey came in, kneeled beside the bed in the dark room, and we talked with my head on the pillow. "The process feels foreign," she empathized. "Once the contractions began, it will feel more familiar."

She offered me Benadryl to sleep. I accepted.

At 4:30 a.m., it was time to check again. No progress. No contractions. No cramps. The nurse started Pitocin through the IV. Slight cramps began.

9 a.m., 11 a.m. No progress. Visitors came. Rebecca Gates visited thrice. Amy Chang visited twice. The second time Amy looked in, the contractions were active. Mid-sentence and mid-contraction, the Foley bulb popped. Amy left. The nurse checked. The bulb was out. That was progress. We watched *Queen of Katwe*. Kyle walked to the cafeteria to buy pizza. When he returned with artichoke and mushroom pizza, it smelled horrible.

By 3 p.m., it seemed active labor began. Stronger contractions required more focus. They slowed again. Active contractions brought peace. When my body grew still, my heart filled with doubt.

At 5 p.m., I asked the daytime resident to check: dilated 5cm, 70% effaced, station -2. The language was familiar. Hope returned. Things were working.

With that, active labor began, full swing. Contractions were intense. I focused during and rested between. Kyle timed them. Every two minutes now. "Good, this is what we're looking for," the doctor said.

I felt the pressure of a baby ready to come into the world. There were no doubts now about our decision to induce. During each painful contraction, I imagined the rise and fall on the monitor. I visualized my body moving her down, closer and closer to us. Soon I would see her. It was a beautiful thing. I felt tranquil. I felt content. Finally, I could do something to help her.

The intensity grew; the moaning began. "Text my mom to come now," I told Kyle.

It was night. Zoey came back on for the night shift.

The urge to push came. She asked to break my water. After a long pause of internal debate, I responded, "No, let's wait."

Through my mind flashed the few statistics via self-report of a better chance of live birth for anencephalic babies if the bag of waters was intact. With a push, the stubborn bag of waters exploded in the room with impressive range.

My body shook. Zoey explained the shaking happened because of the release of hormones like at the end of labor. The contractions stopped. Celeste was +1 station. Zoey called her by name. My cervix was no longer fully open. Zoey said this is normal. "Your body's memory will kick in and take over." I laid down and waited.

Perhaps standing would help move Celeste lower. The contractions were painful. I moaned. After enduring one contraction I laid down again, dozing off between them. The contractions picked up.

The nurse said, "You can push whenever you want." Surely the urge would start again soon. Zoey returned to the room. "I never felt the urge to push," I explained.

The nurse misunderstood.

Zoey sat quietly on the bed. The urge to push never came.

Twice in those moments, I felt Celeste move inside me. She was still alive. I felt grateful for her movement. Every movement was a jolt without the water to cushion it.

Zoey encouraged me to push, even outside a contraction. I tried. She applied pressure to my cervix to simulate the urge to push. It helped and I began. She helped Celeste move forward. Celeste was in the most painful place. Zoey said quietly, "I think one more and we'll get to meet Celeste." It was the ring of fire. I thought of Johnny Cash.

Kyle sat beside me, restless and tired, but fully present. He wanted to hold both my hands. My hand gripped the bed and Kyle's hand as I lay on my side. We locked eyes during contractions. He lifted my leg up to give Celeste room.

Another terrible contraction came. In the middle of it, I felt a strange bliss and light inside me.

An involuntary smile crossed my lips.

With pushing, her head came. Breathe. Rest. Continue pushing. The contractions had all but stopped at this point. With the same loud scream that ushered all my children into the world, Celeste was born. The sweet relief of labor ending overcame me.

Coming to my senses, I struggled to ask, "Is she alive?"

Busy at their end, Zoey responded carefully, "We aren't sure. We need to check her heartbeat." They checked her heartbeat.

The nurse and Zoey covered Celeste's head and lay her gray naked body on me. She was dead. Her limbs flopped. Nothing held her up. My arms weakened. She was not alive, the doctor confirmed. I wept and wailed, "I cannot hold her!"

She is dead.

This is agony.

The nurse quickly took Celeste to clean and dress her. I cried in Kyle's arms. "She was alive!" Yes, just moments ago. Not long ago we heard her heartbeat. Not long ago I felt her move. Was it that moment? That joy? That strange feeling?

Now, I felt ready to hold her. The feeling grew desperate. I craned my neck to look where they had her and asked for her. Sitting up, I cradled her body in my arms. Her skin was pink and not gray. She was dressed in her perfect dress and swaddled in the cozy, colorful, warm blanket my sister made. Celeste and I were close together.

The words echoed in my mind, *the Lord gives and the Lord takes away. Blessed be the name of the Lord. We accept good things from God, should we also not accept evil?*[1]

With my finger, I touched her fingers, her arm, her cheek. I folded the blanket back to see her dress. Kyle and I passed her back and forth as I struggled with cramps. Kyle was immersed in her. He cried. It crushed him that he could not baptize her. He could do nothing for her. Through his tears, I heard him say, "I'm tired of people dying." He faced so much loss this year.

---

[1] Job 1:21 and Job 2:10.

I took pictures with my phone because the nurse was not taking pictures like I thought she would. It was so late: 10 p.m.

Miriam must be told. Like a broken record I called for her.

The nurse went out to get our family. The kids who were awake rushed over to see Celeste. She was not alive. Miriam was crestfallen. Taken aback by the sight of her, James exclaimed three times, "She's so small!" Regina slept in my father's arms. Peter slept in the stroller.

Miriam asked to hold Celeste. She sat on the bed, and I handed Celeste to Miriam. The weight of her lifeless body shook Miriam and she handed Celeste back to me, "She's too heavy."

As my mother held Celeste, Miriam began to cry. Physical weakness crippled me. Kyle held Miriam in his arms. She wanted Celeste to be alive. Miriam would not come to me because of the medical wires and tubing. In this terrible situation, those medical things frightened her. On Peter, they never bothered her.

My mom was sad. Erin came in, fresh off the plane from South Dakota. We were all together. I wanted Erin to see Celeste. I wanted my friend to be here to share this experience so that when I talk about it with her, she was there.

Miriam sat on the stool at the foot of the bed. "I wanted her to hold my finger," she began to cry again. "I'm sad when the things I want to happen don't happen." Could I have put my sadness in any better terms? I wanted Celeste to be born alive.

Everything was planned perfectly. Fr. Raphael was there. Our family was there. Our kids were there. But Celeste was not there. She was gone to the angels. I think I knew the moment she died. "The moment her angel touched your body," Kyle said, "because she was inside your body."

The hour was late. Emotion overwhelmed Miriam too much to hold Celeste now. James refused to sit for a picture. He stayed across the room from Celeste. Peter was stirring from his sleep in the stroller. What else could we do? We sent them back to Family House. "Do you want to sleep with us or go to Family House?" I asked Miriam. Maybe I wanted her with me.

"Go to Family House," she answered.

I laid down to rest.

After Kyle held Celeste for a long time, he murmured, "I'm surprised how much I want to hold her."

He handed her back to me and went to the bathroom to dress for bed. I cradled her in the crook of my arm, as my other newborns lay. While Kyle dressed in the bathroom, I spoke to my little girl. "I wanted you. I love you. You are beautiful."

It was our moment together.

I stroked her hand. Her fingers began to stiffen. There was so much silence in that little body. It was not supposed to be this way. There should be noise and buzzing and nursing and squirming and changing diapers even when its torture to move. Here, there was an immense silence. I took several pictures in this quiet, intimate moment.

Upon returning, Kyle took her up again in his arms, rocking with her back and forth in the rocking chair. The nurse took care of me. Her name was Thea. Thea means God. When Thea was done, Kyle walked back over and whispered, "She's cold." He offered to let me hold her again, but I did not want to. I wanted to keep my perfect moment in mind. We requested Thea take Celeste from the room. She was gone.

We fell asleep exhausted. At 4:30 a.m., Thea returned. It was time for me to empty my bladder. Successful at the first attempt, I climbed back into bed and saw the bassinet behind the curtain at the door. They laid my baby there, and she is not here. The words played again and again.

When I could no longer stifle the sound, Kyle woke. He crawled out of the sleeper chair to come over to me. "Please move that…anywhere." I pleaded.

Though I was calm, it was hard to sleep. Tears came intermittently. Drifting into sleep, the day shift, nurses and Zoey returned. "I want to hold Celeste again…but…I'm worried how she will look," I admitted.

Zoey offered sympathetically, "If she looks similar to how she did the night before, I will bring her back."

Thirty minutes later, the nurse came in with Celeste. I thought they would warn me. Responding to my surprise, Thea asked, "You wanted to hold her, right?"

I stammered, "Ho-how does she look?"

"She is more solid," Thea answered placing her in my arms.

My tiny baby feels like a rock, stiff, heavy, and gray. The pink in her skin is gone. My body repulsed. *I can't see her like this! I cannot hold her.* With renewed tears, I asked Thea to take her. Kyle did not want to hold her, not like this.

Now that it was day, the nurse offered to bring in a professional photographer. I looked again at my cell phone photos from the night before. *Let me keep the image of Celeste I knew last night.* It was enough.

We did what we could to begin the day. Miriam asked my mom if she could see Celeste. Adrienne, the Child Life

Specialist, offered to look at Celeste to discern if the change might be too much for Miriam. I suspected it was. "Would you like to go with her?" I asked my mom. She and my dad went with Adrienne. The nurse dressed Celeste in white pajamas with delicate roses and returned her dress to us. I will never see her in those pajamas. Miriam and Regina wore those pajamas. All my daughters wore those pajamas.

The group returned. My mom nodded her head with eyes full of sorrow and silence. It would be too much for the children. With Adrienne, they painted a rock to celebrate Celeste.

Waves of tears and calm, and bright moments filled the day. Once I decided I did not want to stay another night, they rushed us out sooner than I was ready for. When the woman from transport wheeled me out in a wheelchair, I saw a warmer and began to cry. I was leaving my baby.

I am going, and she is not with me.

The woman from transport opened the doors to a hallway lined with warmers. "Let's go a different way," she said quickly, redirecting my chair. Kyle held my hand.

My heart ached as we passed the waiting room to the elevator. When I was there last, Celeste was with me, alive.

The tears came again as I waited for Kyle to get the van. Adrienne passed by and spoke with me. Our chatting about the other children was a distraction and a comfort. Only periodic tears affected me on the way home. I reviewed the moments again and again. Never forget.

She was born at 9:34 p.m. She weighed 4 lbs., 9 ounces. Her body was too small for tissue donation. She is my baby.

The email to family and friends who all prayed intensely that she might be born alive was not difficult to write:

Celeste Casey was born around 10 p.m. on March 2, 2017, with beautiful lips, long fingers, and perfect baby toes. She was stillborn. While we might be tempted to sing with the Scarecrow, "if she only had a brain" better still we sing with Job, "the Lord gives, the Lord takes away, blessed be the name of the Lord...We accept good things from God, should we not also accept evil?"

We thank you for the prayers and support you have given. They were indeed felt, and I am sure will continue to be.

The recovery was not as painful as my other deliveries, probably because, as James said, she was so small. Miriam and I spent the evening together talking about her. I edited the photos and wrote everything I could remember in order to hold it all in mind. Friends visited.

Some well-intentioned people told me I would feel empty following her death. It did not feel that way. Maybe I would later. It felt like we were celebrating Celeste. We were sad, but Miriam and I talked a great deal about her. That felt good.

Chapter 18

Holy Saturday

Now in the place where he had been crucified there was a garden, and in the garden a new tomb... (John 19:41)

Taking the body, Joseph wrapped it [in] clean linen and laid it in his new tomb that he had hewn in the rock. Then he rolled a huge stone across the entrance to the tomb and departed. But Mary Magdalene and the other Mary remained sitting there, facing the tomb. (Matthew 27:59-61)

With my heart, I photographed those days. Every hour changed the lighting.

After birth: sad but at peace, at times able to engage, laugh and smile. Mental images stayed before me, visualizing her at UCSF, feeling she was safe. Sometimes strangely composed about everything, marveling at how I was not depressed or lost.

Erin stayed with us and took care of everything around the house. She was quick to care for the children so Kyle and I could be in our fog. I laid in bed, wishing I was out of bed. Each evening, Erin joined me, and we talked about politics, relationships, childrearing and religion. She was a light to me in those dark days.

Sunday, March 5: Another woman at church had her baby. Her belly grew these past months as mine did. They took their baby girl home. I wished I could have taken my baby girl home. My heart throbbed to care for Celeste. It was senseless to recover from the childbirth of a child I do not have. My hands gripped the pew for support after communion under the weight of heartache.

Monday, March 6: The milk came in, and the aching continued. I was sad. My eyes were swollen from last night's tears. Kyle and I talked about the images we held. Kyle said he rocked her and thought of how he would never be able to rock her to sleep, but there, he rocked her into eternal sleep. He wanted to sing a lullaby but could not get the words out. Kyle held her hand and felt her grow cold. It made sense.

My moment was holding her as I held my co-sleeping babies, by my side, feeling the warmth and softness of her blanket. Now I felt depressed and wished for routine and activity. I wanted to talk to Summer.

Joanna visited from Washington State to be here for us. She bought cabbage and licorice tea to help decrease the milk and pain. Licorice tea was the best part I remember from those days.

My sister flew from Kansas. Both had to leave before the funeral. Swollen with unneeded milk, my breasts hurt their worst the afternoon I saw my sister. She left soon after helping my parents watch the children while we made funeral arrangements.

Wednesday, March 8: Today's reflection, Celeste went from the warmth of my womb to the arms of the father.

Thursday, March 9: Tori emailed this hymn to me:

> Be still, my soul; the Lord is on thy side;
> Bear patiently the cross of grief or pain;
> Leave to thy God to order and provide;

In every change, He faithful will remain.
Be still, my soul; thy best, thy heavenly, Friend
Through thorny ways leads to a joyful end.[1]

Miriam seemed to be processing well. The first days we combed through the white textured box of Celeste's things prepared by the hospital. How carefully we tied the white satin ribbon each time we finished. Wednesday, we passed photos back and forth and I asked how she feels. "Happy," she said.

Today, Kyle took a blanket and a Hello Kitty doll (a gift from Miriam) to Celeste. We gave our kisses and hugs to the baby blanket Miriam and Regina used as infants for Celeste to take with her. We are not ancient Egyptians filling the sarcophagus. I knew she could not feel it, but still, I did not want her to be cold.

In the afternoon, we went to spend time with Celeste. We took pictures in the room with the closed-lid casket from the Trappist monks. At the end, I put my hands on top of her casket. My heart surged within me. She came from my body. How connected my body was to hers. How desperately I wanted to open that lid.

We had to leave. My heart ripped out. *My baby!*

But Mary did not stay at the tomb. She had faith in the resurrection. The thought fortified me to leave.

There was a phone call on the way home. Because of permits, it might not be possible to bury her in the morning. *Oh, God, why!*

---

[1] Von Schlegel, Kathraina; 1855. "Be Still, my Soul." Trans. by Jane Borthwick. https://hymnary.org/text/be_still_my_soul_the_lord_is_on_thy_side

I want my baby! A cloud of darkness covered me. I was desperate for her.

The feeling of her inside me was still fresh. The wounds not yet healed.

Before Celeste was born, Erin emailed this poem to me. The poem played on repeat in my mind.

ENOUGH ! we're tired, my heart and I.
We sit beside the headstone thus,
And wish that name were carved for us.[2]

March 10, Friday, the funeral, and burial: The morning hurt. It went in slow motion. With bold lipstick, I tried to distract from my swollen eyes. I did not want it to be this way. It should not be happening. Mass felt like it went on forever. Dina and her son sang. He muddled the words in "O God Beyond All Praising," but I felt them and cried them just the same.

People liked the eulogy. It felt as if Kyle held me up as we walked to the lectern and I read those words.

We drove to the burial. My heart burst anew when they lowered her casket. *Let me stay!*

My mother laid tulips on her grave. How pretty the vibrant crimson, violet and ivory looked against the redwood. The casket was made at a monastery and a redwood tree was planted for Celeste there.

How I wanted to help my children, but the fog persisted.

---

[2] Browning, Elizabeth and Robert Browning. *The Love Poems of Elizabeth and Robert Browning.* "My Heart and I" Edited by Louis Untermeyer. (New York: Barnes and Noble Books, 1994), 34.

But when we came to the reception at my mother's house, I was ready to move forward. A rainbow of colorful fruits and vegetables with cheese and crackers from YLI, and potted ranunculus and tulips from my mother dressed the countertops and tables. Instead of talking about Celeste, I interrogated my cousin about his job prospects.

March 11: I am grateful she is at rest. It was Kyle's birthday.

> On the seventh day, the child died. And the servants of David were afraid to tell him that the child was dead; for they said, "While the child was still alive, we spoke to him, and he did not listen to us; how then can we tell him the child is dead? He may do himself some harm." But when David saw that his servants were whispering together, he perceived that the child was dead; and David said to his servants, "Is the child dead?" They said, "He is dead."
> Then David rose from the ground, washed, anointed himself, and changed his clothes. He went into the house of the Lord, and worshiped; he then went to his own house; and when he asked, they set food before him and he ate. Then his servants said to him, "What is this thing that you have done? You fasted and wept for the child while it was alive; but when the child died, you rose and ate food." He said, "While the child was still alive, I fasted and wept; for I said, 'Who knows? The Lord may be gracious to me, and the child may live.' But now he is dead; why should I fast? Can I bring him back again? I shall go to him, but he will not return to me." (2 Samuel 12: 18-23)

March 12, Sunday: Outside St. Joseph's while the children ate donuts, I faced my first question, "How's your little baby?"

Did "baby" mean Celeste or Peter? What was said was said. I began to cry. Sugey deflected by saying, "She's asking about Peter." We talked about Peter instead. The time to answer that question will come, probably tomorrow. Still, I faced it.

We survived.

The Eulogy
written while Celeste kicked inside

Man cannot truly find himself, except through a sincere gift of self.

We learned from John Paul II that to love truly is not only to will the good of the beloved but also to be willing to give of oneself, to sacrifice oneself, to that end. There is no title or status change when a parent loses a child. Until recent history and place, parenthood was synonymous with loss. Indeed, it still is. From birth when they are no longer protected in the womb, to the first time they fall, to the two-year-old insistence that only one parent may help with shoes, to the four-year urge for independence "I can do it myself" to the age when they really and truly can. Or, more painfully, the first illness, the first injury, the first hospital visit, and the first terrible day when you think of what could have happened, and thankfully did not.

A year and a half ago, we faced for the first time, the knowledge that a child of ours would have a birth defect. Following the birth of Peter Solanus Casey, we faced our first NICU visit, first ER visit, first long hospital stay, first fear of losing our child, first surgeries, first inherited genetic mutation, and first understanding that this could have happened with any of our children and future children. But we also faced our first cleft smile, which is the biggest and brightest full-faced smile you can imagine, first easy going baby, first baby to self-soothe bringing some much needed nighttime relief. No cup of suffering came without the relief and joy of meeting this boy and knowing him and living with him in our family.

We were changed by these early experiences. Armed with the strength of the previous year, we learned of a diagnosis much worse than what we already knew. At 18 weeks pregnant, I could see the sonogram images were not as they should be. Our baby girl had anencephaly, a condition that develops in the early weeks of pregnancy, in which the child does not grow a brain. In my womb, she could continue to grow to full term, be born naturally, and then pass peacefully away. Guided by the Catholic Church's teaching, we came to understand her life should not be cut short. Over the course of pregnancy, Celeste Casey became part of the fabric of this family. "Celeste in mommy's tummy" entered the canon of toddler speech. To their joy or bewilderment, the older children felt her kick. We experienced an even greater outpouring of love than we had already known.

There has been much grieving in this family this year. In the summer, the loss of a Theresa Parma, who lived a long-lived life surrounded by 3 children, 13 grandchildren and 13 great-grandchildren. In the winter, the untimely death of Trevor Casey, a man full of potential and love. And now it is spring, and now the death of Celeste Casey who went from the peace and security of the womb straight to the arms of the Father to join her two other siblings lost through miscarriage. With the saints of God, she will pray for this family, she will care for us, as we ached to care for her.

Richard John Neuhaus wrote, "At the heart of darkness the hope of the world is dying on a cross, and the longest stride of the soul is to see in this a strange glory... The cross is not the eclipse of that glory but its shining forth, its epiphany."[3]

There is no title for a parent who has lost a child. The grief that comes with faithfulness is built into the definition of mother and father.

We will walk forward in the mystery of life with the joy and suffering that it brings, and will one day, in the hope of God, find meaning in it all.

---

[3] Neuhaus, Richard John. 2001, 91. *Death on a Friday Afternoon: Meditations on the Last Words of Jesus from the Cross*. New York: Basic Books.

Part IV

The Glorious Mysteries

Chapter 19

Waiting for the Resurrection: The Trauma of the Cross

And they said to her, "Woman, why are you weeping?" She said to them, "They have taken my Lord, and I don't know where they laid him." When she had said this, she turned around and saw Jesus there, but did not know it was Jesus. Jesus said to her, "Woman, why are you weeping? Whom are you looking for?" She thought it was the gardener and said to him, "Sir, if you carried him away, tell me where you laid him, and I will take him." (John 20: 13-16)

"When I closed the eyes of my dear little children and when I buried them, I felt great pain, but it was always with resignation. I didn't regret the sorrows and the problems I had endured for them. Several people said to me, 'It would be better to never have had them.' I can't bear that kind of talk. I don't think the sorrows and problems could be weighed against the eternal happiness of my children. So they weren't lost forever. Life is short and full of misery. We'll see them again in Heaven. Above all, it was on the death of my first child that I felt more deeply the happiness of having a child in Heaven, for God showed me in a noticeable way that He accepted my sacrifice. Through the intercession of my little angel, I received a very extraordinary grace,"[1]

The end of March came. Time moved away from the worst moments of our lives.

---

[1] Martin, Zelie and Louis Martin. 2011, 90. *A Call to a Deeper Love: The Family Correspondence of the Parents of St. Thérèse of the Child Jesus 1863-1885*. Edited by Dr. Frances Renda. Translated by Anne Connors Hess. New York: St. Paul's.

Joy returned as well. At the end of the homily, Fr. Raju said a prayer, first in his native Indian tongue, then in English, "Lead me, Lord, from death to life."

This was what I begged of God, to share with me the God I knew him to be, to lift me up again. As the prayers took place and communion commenced, my mind was absorbed in an image of the story I wrote in my youth.

It played out thus: the girl woke up, and, this time, she was not alone. The king was with her, and with him was Celeste, not as an infant, but a grown woman, breathtakingly beautiful and somehow greater in stature and more knowing than the girl herself. The girl was not alone.

Then God spoke to me.

> "I love you;
> > I am with you;
> > > I never left you;
> > > > I will always be with you."

Celeste felt close. She felt near me ever since that moment. Free from sorrow, my eyes rested on the photograph of her face. She is still within reach. It may be that the freedom I felt from sorrow allowed Miriam's spirits to lower. Once a day, she cried thinking of Celeste. Our feelings did not align. My mind turned toward the sky.

When we returned home from the hospital I had to rest, to cope, to keep it together. After imbibing too much a few nights in a row, I wanted to find other ways to cope. The key ingredients for a day of sanity consisted of licorice tea, reading David Copperfield and Cut Flower Farm, walking, and planning projects for my home. Bonus activities included arranging flowers, completing said projects, an hour phone call with Summer each week.

On Thursday, I read to my children. On Friday, we prayed the Stations of the Cross at home. Attending to them, I took their needs into my mind and parented them. It felt marvelous. On Saturday, we shopped at the Farmer's Market. The children waited as I stared at the flowers at the Kelley Flower Farm stand and chatted with Sharon. That may have been Thursday or Saturday. The days blurred together. On Sunday at 5 a.m., a month after Celeste died, Peter's temperature was 103.

Quick as I could, I packed and rushed him to the local hospital. My husband stayed behind to prepare the children. It was Sunday. Peter must be admitted, and our family must have our weekend visit. Everyone arrived at UCSF around the same time, Peter and I in an ambulance, Kyle with the kids in the van.

When they left Tuesday morning, it was clear we would stay. What must I do to keep myself going? There was a time when I longed for the city because there, I knew how to cope. Peter was safe there. Now I wished to be home because there I knew how to cope. Home felt safe. It was time to erase the geography from the equation and take to heart Summer's words: the ability to do this is in me.

I walked, I read and I wrote. When I wrote, the gladness returned. The writing was fun.

On Tuesday, two gentlemen in navy coveralls pruned the plants in Mariposa Park while the musky floral fragrance filled the air. Without shyness, I approached and asked if I could take some cuttings. He gave me his clippers and I took a small batch of flowers. On Wednesday, a man sold orchids at the Mission Bay Farmer's Market. I purchased a lemon colored orchid in honor of Regina's favorite color.

I walked. I read. I wrote. I worried.

Peter grew worse, and so I wrote more. The situation was outside my control. Through a thin veil of fiction, I explored my heart.

"DIC."[2]

"Non-cultured sepsis."

"Micro-clotting."

There were too many new words this time, too many new concepts. Doctors from immunology visited multiple times as Peter's hemoglobin dropped. Medical professionals replenished him with blood products. There may be another disorder, one that causes the immune system to attack itself.

"HLH."[3]

It is treated with a dose of steroids that makes a mother's heart cry. Peter lay there. These were the days of March and September come back to us. My son was sick and lay beyond my reach.

For thirty minutes in the morning and thirty minutes in the afternoon, Peter sat up to play. On the floor mat, we played with shapes and buckets. He reached out to me. It seemed like he wanted to stand. He toddled toward me, and dropped into my arms, crying. Then he went to sleep or lay listless with his eyes open. The pattern repeated in the evening, and twice the next day. They announced they would move him to the PICU.

---

[2] Disseminated intravascular coagulation (DIC) is a rare and serious condition that disrupts your blood flow. It is a blood clotting disorder that can turn into uncontrollable bleeding.

[3] Hemophagocytic Lymphohistiocystosis, a life-threatening disease of severe hyperinflammation.

How I hated the PICU. It was desperation, illness, fog and fear.

While we waited for transport, with my weak child in my arms, looking at Sharon, I quietly pleaded, "Sharon..." She came to me, hugged me and told me all the ways Peter was doing okay. "He is alert; he is listening; he is responding; he is crying out."

Only partially did I understand her words. The depth of loss ate at my heart while I felt my son slip away.

Dr. Duncan Henry, the attending physician, is my friend now. He guided the crib downstairs as Sharon and I walked alongside Peter. My hands clutched the potted orchid and plastic cup of cut flowers. Plants were not allowed in the PICU.

As Dr. Henry wheeled the crib around the corner of the hallway, under that PICU sign, my breathing overwhelmed me.

It increased rapidly. It was a panic attack. As I stopped walking, Dr. Henry sent Sharon ahead with Peter and stood beside me while I held the corner of the wall and closed my eyes. He talked me through and asked me questions. Did he perceive what I was feeling?

When I could breathe again, my feet transported me in slowly. Falling was not an option.

Amy Chang visited, and Dr. Henry left us to talk. We sat at the table by the wall, behind the activity. This was where Kyle and I spent our days of shock a year before. To only Amy, I could ask these questions. "If things continue, what will happen?"

I could only see from this spot to death. What lay in between?

"If things got worse, he would stop responding, stop crying, he would not react differently to you than others."

"Would you tell me...in enough time...if I needed to call Kyle to come?" If there were only a few moments left, I wanted Kyle to be there. Afraid to ask, but more afraid of the unknown, I had to face this.

"Yes," Amy spoke definitively. The force in her voice strengthened me.

Dr. Posner walked in, and Amy brought her into the conversation. Amy is aware of what Amanda means to me. Dr. Posner's words implied some major shift occurs when the doctors think it is time to call home. They would not say it lightly. Then the two began to encourage me to call Kyle for support. Maybe I should not be alone. If Peter was the same tomorrow, I would call.

Before Amanda Posner left...for her, Peter sat up.

Just as surely as we faced the clouds, the storm turned around.

He spent the next 12 hours annoying the PICU nurse by playfully throwing his toys on the ground and tangling his leads. The fair-haired doctor from hematology told me through her surgical mask that Peter does not have HLH because patients with HLH cannot improve on their own. After one more day, we returned to where we belonged, on the 5th floor, Transitional Care Unit.

Peter was himself again. We arrived in time to hold Regina's April 8th birthday party in the T-CUP with buckets of munchies, water with straws and irises from the garden that smelled like burnt rubber. The children helped me carry strawberry shortcake to the nurses and doctors on the floor.

Fr. Raphael told me a story while we stood outside Peter's door.

There were men carrying crosses up a mountain. One group complained of the weight of the cross, so they stopped halfway up, still complaining. The other group continued on. The first group got an idea to make it easier. They cut the length of their crosses so they would not be so heavy. Thus they continued on.

The second group, farther up, reached a river without a bridge. The angel told them, "Lay down your cross to act as a bridge. Then, once on the other side, pick up your cross and carry on."

And so they did.

When the second group reached the river, the angel gave the same directions: lay down your cross to act as a bridge.

But, when they laid their crosses down, the crosses fell into the river and washed away, because they were too short to bridge the river. And so the group was stuck.

"The cross is the bridge to that strange glory."

Peter was stable now. We went home.

Waves of relief washed over me each time we returned home from UCSF, permitting the belief it was over to settle in. We are home now. Settling in made each return a jolt.

That mindset caused me to lose my peace. It took 12 months of our hospital life (which started when he was two-months-old) before I learned a new way of looking at it. It came to me through a story.

We are going up a mountain, hiking on a switchback trail. On one side is the verdant meadow, the sweet relief, the promise of comfort and ease, the time with family, my beautiful home, the good health of my boy. On the other side, it is dry and dusty and dead because this mountain is a volcano in California. And we walk, back and forth, up, up, up. Sometimes we face the meadow, sometimes we face the dry side. But it will change. Whichever side we are on, it will change.

In a moment, the thought changed everything.

How would I apply the coping skills I learned in the hospital to my life lived at home? With the demands of home, it would look different, but serve me the same. Walk in the evening when my husband got home or exercise when I first wake. Stretch. Read before bed. Try to unplug. Try to eat healthily, feed myself as healthily as I try to feed my children. Try to avoid the mindset that I deserve this sweet or I deserved this drink and focus on ways that will actually lower my stress. Ask my existential questions and seek out spiritual and emotional support. Talk to my husband. Craft.

The reward at home is greater because I was in my artful home that I lovingly crafted. The joy was greater because when I put my computer aside and watched the children march around the house with instruments, with Peter crawling after them, my heart swelled. As he crawled, he had a g-tube and Broviac under that shirt. We will change his dressing in a couple days and, with a syringe, infuse vitamins into his TPN that night before connecting him to a 1.5-liter bag of mystery stuff that makes him grow.

All this I knew. It did not matter.

These are the perfectly imperfect moments. Learning to live in and enjoy the moment, coping and caring for myself, staying aware of my interior life as well as my exterior life. These are things I have learned. Each month I may have to learn them all over again. But we keep moving forward.

The lesson came home to me when I reflected on the day of Regina's birthday party in the hospital, watching the children eat picnic food out of summer buckets. The imperfect moments become perfect when we are all together. It did not matter that it was cramped, undecorated or improvised, so long as we were together. We are connected to Celeste by the invisible string. Soon it will be Easter...and we are all together!

The joy I felt in Peter's energy made the trying steps of coping seem unnecessary. The Internet habits, television habits and alcohol habits—all the self-medicating habits returned.

Time to learn again. Time to pick up the book I read daily at the hospital. Time to write again. Time to pray again. It might make me more flexible. It would make me happier. So much of it was simply the decision to do. It was a decision to do the things we knew we should but feel too lazy to do. The temptation was to vegetate or numb, but that does not help. It was time to step forward.

Chapter 20

Easter Sunday

Jesus said to her, "Mary!" She turned and said to him in Hebrew, "Rabbouni," which means Teacher. Jesus said to her, "Stop holding on to me, for I have not yet ascended to the Father. But go to my brothers and tell them, 'I am going to my Father and your Father, to my God and your God.'" (John 20: 16-17)

I protected myself by exercising in the afternoon, walking in the evening and reading at night. Three laps around the park cleared my head from the post-naptime onslaught of crying and screaming by hell-bound ruffians, my blessed children. Emotional survival felt like a tedious process until a great excitement came along. And excitement did come: Easter.

We had such a day planned! Holy Saturday was spent in a delicious frenzy implementing plans brewing in my mind for months. Earlier this year, I made bunting using a stained thrift-store crocheted tablecloth, cut into triangles and sewn by machine to two-inch baby pink grosgrain ribbon. I sewed two, one for the fireplace mantle and one for the bay window behind our dining table.

Inside the dusty box of Easter decorations buried in a mess of artificial flowers, I unearthed a pair of ceramic Pottery Barn rabbits and birds' nests, loads of birds' nests from our former home in the middle of nowhere called Owl Creek. The longer stems became a wreath around the dining table pendant light.

A pink floral table runner bought on a whim in our first year of marriage, covered the seam of our newly made pastel pink tablecloth. Kelley Flower Farm blush peonies and Dusty Miller combined with Trader Joe's tulips stood in a white vase atop disks of almond wood from my father's orchard. The plan came to life quickly and beautifully.

The children decorated Easter baskets using ribbon, hot glue and artificial flowers from the dollar store. They called the shots; I stuck the glue. The children set them out at night and found them filled in the morning with books, treats and garden tools.

When I settled into bed, I anticipated the kids would wake, discover the Easter baskets and ravage the poor things. Bowls of cereal would await the hunter-gatherers. Then we would head to mass and return for egg hunting. Festivities would continue with Easter Brunch at our house feasting on cucumber and tomato salad, berry citrus fruit salad, breakfast strata, Italian Easter bread and raspberry sorbet.

After naps, the party would move to my parent's house, where my introverted husband would prepare a dinner of deviled eggs, carrot ginger soup, roasted green beans with caramelized pecans, rack of lamb with pomegranate and fennel glaze served with St. Francis Cabernet Sauvignon. The meal would conclude with Farmer's Market strawberries, three-year aged cheddar and crème brulée.

Unlike every event I remembered from the past year, nearly every plan took effect. Easter proceeded much as I anticipated, idyllic in every way.

Once Easter Sunday passed, the heart-turmoil of Monday returned. Fear of the unknown sent me spiraling downward. It seemed impossible to talk or pay attention to my children. Kyle was home. In a trance, I mulled around avoiding Peter as much as I could. He was sick, but likely with a cold. There was nothing I recognized as too dangerous, but we do not call him, "Sneaky Pete" for nothing.

My trauma hit me in the head like a 2×4. It was the trauma of what happened one year before, the trauma that happened one week before, the trauma that happens when, the first time you see your baby, you understand she is dead.

The fear paralyzed me.

Then he was fine. Nothing happened; nothing changed.

His labs showed he was a little more dehydrated. His doctor hypothesized why he lost fluid, but we passed a normal week at home with him crawling around the place like he owned it, eager to find and follow his siblings running fast.

Fear that day was big and out-of-control. All the peace I once possessed left me. *How can I learn to stay cool when these things come up?* This was exposure therapy. If I worked through the worry, I could learn to not let the trauma control me.

"Searching for and Maintaining Peace: A Small Treatise on Peace of Heart" a book written by Jacques Philippe,[1] whispered my thoughts. Camille recommended that book. All this time, it remained nestled between other bigger and better-used books.

The author wrote that perhaps the goal of spiritual combat is not to be invincible and victorious. Maybe, for those who seek to follow the will of God, it is to maintain our peace in all things. We are weak enough. At times, we will fall into temptation, sin, mistakes, but God calls us not to

---

[1] Jacques Phillipe, *Searching for and Maintaining Peace* (New York: Brothers of the Society of St. Paul, 2002), 12.

fret too much about it. He calls us to pick up and keep moving.

Is this not what God has been asking, with each turn Peter takes, that I adapt and maintain peace to get through it? Is it not the project I saw with each new set of bad news, with each return to the hospital? We traveled back and forth, requiring more and more flexibility, and more and more understanding. We ought not to look to flip the switch and wake up, but simply to turn the corner and persevere.

Peter threw up again, and I waited for the doctor to call. He continued to play. All signs indicated he was probably okay. We would cover our bases. Stay calm and attentive in this. The fear of the unknown need not paralyze me.

The turn came.

We drove again to the Emergency Dept. One time, long ago, Kyle asked me to write down what I knew for functioning in the hospital. After spending 12 hours in the local Emergency Dept. this time, I came up with some clear ideas.

I told him to be comfortable in the Emergency Dept. with a baby is an art form.

Don't feel embarrassed by comments that you brought a lot of baggage.

Bring a lot of baggage:

- Diapers, wipes, and baby clothes
- Food for you and food (as needed) for Peter for at least 6 hours
- A laptop, iPod, Smart phone of whatever technology. There is generally too much noise and baby comforting to focus on a book. Electronics help.
- Magazines so Peter can play with the pages.

- Chargers for devices. Five hours of texting updates will drain the battery.
- A handful of toys and comfort objects.
- A shirt, pair of underwear, and pair of socks, just in case Peter is destined for a chopper ride and I cannot take much with me. UCSF will have the soap and toothbrush.

These items are essential for me. Even in the midst of the emergency that takes me in, it is worth it to gather or have someone gather these things.

A nurse recommended when it's crowded that we stand by the Emergency Dept. entrance after checking in to protect Peter from whatever other lobby-dwellers may be breathing out. His blanket functions as a mask by keeping it near his face, where it comforts him as well.

In the beginning, I suffered from the I-can't-believe-I'm-bringing-my-baby-to-the-hospital whirlwind of thoughts. The key to focus was the here-and-now. After so many visits, I recognize many of the nurses and I focus on remembering more.

When led to our room, I find it best to assume I will live there forever. The Emergency Dept. exists in a time warp where 30 minutes feels like three hours.

The doctor's stool becomes a footrest. It rolls and spins, and is, thus, entertaining. Ask for water.

So many times, I would have liked a crib for Peter. But it's even better to keep the bed in the room in order to lay down. Line one side of the two-foot wide bed with every bag to reduce the risk of Peter falling through the rails. At one visit, during the 3 o'clock morning hour, a nurse revealed I could have asked for a bassinet. During that visit to CHO, it saved my sanity. I slept on the bed.

The pole should be on the same side as you and Peter, so you can stand up and soothe him without being too tightly tethered. When Peter is tired, adjust the lighting. Our local Emergency Dept. no longer uses the call button, so it's anyone's guess how to get help.

The expectation to see the doctor is futile. He thinks he would be right back, but in reality, it will be at least two hours, your time. To him, it feels like four minutes once he leaves the room.

Move often. Stand. Sit. Lay down. Use the bathroom. It has never been hard to find someone to stay with Peter when I need to go to the restroom because he is cute. Ask for food and water before the urge to faint, or as you tell me, before "you're getting there."

I want to be the favorite parent/patient in the Emergency Dept., so I am nice to my nurse. Be nice to the nurse. They know where the coffee is. Learn the nurse's name, and use it when you say "thank you" or "excuse me."

It is important to smile and say please and thank you. When emotionally able, I try to express specific appreciation. It is just good manners. Nurses linger more with pleasant patients. This increases opportunities to ask questions or to express concerns that are harder to recall during swift interactions.

It is best if I assume staff will tell nothing of what they are doing. Ask the doctors: "What tests do you plan to do...how long will it take those tests to result?"

Otherwise, they may not tell you, depending on the *modus operandi* of the particular Emergency Dept. and doctor.

"Do you really need that much blood?" There are maximum amounts they are allowed to collect, but I only want them to take the minimum.

Medical jargon harnesses professional respect quickly. Over time questions will intimidate you less. "Why are you running this test? Why are you not running this test?"

It takes time to learn your limits. It hurts to see our baby hurt. We are human, too. Some procedures are too painful to watch.

Along with the time warp, the numbing quality of the beeps, strange lighting and smallness of the room make me lose my mind. It is best to approach time in Emergency Dept. as you would solitary confinement: stay mentally active.

At hour ten, a nurse allowed Peter and I to step outside the doorway where the ambulances pull up. It boosted my morale and patience during the last hour to warm myself in the sun and relatively fresh air. No tubes tethered Peter. No fevers spiked. We waited only for transport.

The goal is to practice all of that. You may be able to do none of it. That's okay. I tell myself, it's okay if I weep, if I hold him, if I worry and forget to remind the nurse to use an alcohol wipe at every step of accessing his Broviac. Regardless, I try to murmur those "please and thank you's" because the staff really is doing all they can. I remind myself that it is okay to leave it to them.

Time and practice strengthened my ability to intervene and ask the question. Sometimes all that strength was directly to the simple act of holding my suffering child. With each difficult time, I grew stronger.

When people met us and asked their questions, they told me I was strong, but I felt weak. We start out weak. Even if we are weak, we will get through it, but we must guard our thoughts against the whirlwind of destructive thoughts. If we crawl out of this experience on our knees, we still got through it.

Once settled in at UCSF, Dr. Rosenthal announced he would not accept an unknown answer to the second admission for repeated fevers. "Two times is two times too much," he stately gruffly. This man was always difficult to talk with, to work with, to share my concerns with. At that moment, he was my hero.

The week passed uneventfully as Peter's fevers subsided. Back and forth across the mountainside, we returned home.

Chapter 21

Ascension Thursday

He answered them, "It is not for you to know the times or seasons that the Father has established by his own authority. But you will receive power when the Holy Spirit comes upon you, and you will be my witnesses in Jerusalem, throughout Judea and Samaria, and to the ends of the earth." When he had said this, as they were looking on, he was lifted up, and a cloud took him from their sight. (Acts 1: 7-9)

Upon reflection, I asked myself, who am I? When she died, I crossed the great distance from before to after.

My world changed. What do I see in this world now?

In this world lurks a darkness I did not recognize before. Because of this, there is a fear I must work through to be able to live day-to-day, the fear my children might not always be here.

There are invisible strings tying me to an unseen world. This is where the light begins. It runs down these strings into my heart and it gives me peace in those times of terrible darkness.

I can see angels now. They were invisible before, but we feel more protected than ever, helped through circumstances that carry us into and out of the darkness.

There is a kinship now with others who have suffered. Those who have suffered view the world differently. The worst thing imaginable can be survived. In many cases, we would do it again if we had to, even it only meant holding the baby for one more moment.

Art makes me come alive in ways that never happened before. The State of California deems my M.S. in Clinical

Psychology useless. But, for Peter's sake, we will not leave California. One professional door closed for the time being, and of all things, the best way for me to contribute financially to my family is through art, through writing. The pressure dissipated. Writing will never pay the student loans the way counseling would have. Thus, I am at leisure. We will pay more than we ever have because there will be no other way to make it happen. In this way, I am no longer waiting. This is a whole new world.

In art, I find beauty and fun. The sadness of grief and the anxiety of fear is bleak and ugly. When I am around beauty and when I arrange or make or create sentences, I feel myself reconnected to that invisible world from whence beauty comes and where it was perfected. There, the world makes sense in a world wrought with mourning and illness and dressing changes.

I am more compassionate, less judgmental, but likely, not more patient. The world moves right along with me in creativity, forming collaboratives and providing peace in a world of uncertainty.

I am an imperfect mother. The physical capability of mothering required of a mother with four kids slowly returned. The mental capability grew. The emotional capability has yet to be determined. I may not be better than I was.

Thursdays changed fundamentally for me. Every week at the cemetery was different.

The first Thursday, I stressed over what flowers to take her. They had to be right. They must not die quickly. When I arrived with potted ranunculus, my body relaxed with a sigh of relief to be near her body again. Things were as they should be. A mother's body is meant to be near the body of her baby. I wished I could see her, hold her, have her with me alive. It is impossible this side of heaven. Being near provided much relief.

The second time I fussed over peonies and trying to get to the grave on Thursday. In my mind, it had to be Thursday. Thursday was the day she died. Thursday, I had to be with her. We went as a family this time. We took her irises from the garden and spent time there. We were all together. It was like the strange peace in the private room of the funeral home, with her in her casket. We did not see her, but being together, things felt right in a way they no longer did on the outside.

The other Thursdays blended together. On one Thursday it took forever to get out the door. Then I remembered to take the roses. Then this. Then that. By the time we were graveside, we had just ten minutes before needing to rush off. Another Thursday I made plans for lunch. With the Farmers' Market bouquet, but little else, time moved quickly.

Then came the Thursday I was gone. In San Francisco with Peter in the hospital, I could not go to her grave. My mother and daughter went in my stead with "Papoo's roses" as we call them, roses grown from a plant my mother purchased after her father died. No one went the following Thursday. It was a sweet relief to get back there again. There were no flowers that Thursday.

The Thursdays became less important. The flowers became less important. Still, I visited on Thursday. Still, I brought flowers.

On one Thursday, I went agitated and ill at ease. An SUV was parked beside her grave. I knelt on the pavement, beside the wheel of the SUV, and met the mother of two boys buried next to Celeste as she finished her cigarette.

We talked a little in between my tears.

I thought I would feel some bond if I met another mother there. There was no great affection. Summer said I have chosen not to take my identity in being the mother of a deceased infant. That is true. There is a lot more to my life. Days like today, on Thursday, life and death define me. The mother left. After moving my car, I sat in silence. Peace returned.

A quiet spirit is not only found in the cemetery. I review the lesson in my mind. She is in Heaven. She is not here. In my mind's eye, I see her with her soul fully-formed appearing to me like a woman in Heaven, complete and full of joy.

This little body in the ground is not all of her. That which makes her is in Heaven. There are no walls between Heaven and me, so she can be with me, just not the way I wish she could be on Thursdays.

Today, without planning, I bought a small bunch of dahlias at the Farmer's Market. The moment I placed them in that cemetery vase filled with water from the sprinklers, I felt a ray of light in my heart. This is my gift to her. How satisfying it felt to give her something when it feels I can give her nothing. I stayed a little and felt the peace of God. *It is good that I am here.*

I left...rather determined to hold my friend's newborn. It was not like holding her. How still that sleeping baby was. How still my girl was when I held her. It was not the same. A mother cannot feel the same for someone else's child as she can her own. Still, I was proud I dared to hold an infant again.

The rest of the day was a little unproductive and a little less patient. But I allowed it. It was Thursday, after all.

Chapter 22

The Coming of the Holy Spirit

"The Advocate, the Holy Spirit that the Father will send in my name—he will teach you everything and remind you of all that [I] told you. Peace I leave with you; my peace I give to you. Not as the world gives do I give it to you. Do not let your hearts be troubled or afraid." (John 14:26-27)

When the going gets rough at home, I think about returning to San Francisco. In the quiet, routine, reflective time, I know myself better.

For the first time, since this crisis began, I told Kyle, "I want you to come with me." Without discussion, without question, I told him we should be together. He came. Peter was admitted again.

The children stayed with my parents. We drove separately. His presence gave me more time for reflection and time for us to think about being a couple again.

Walking home to Family House after a day of occupying Peter, my heart sank as the sound of a chopper filled the air and I perceived the reflection of its lights in the glass housing above Subway. It sank to realize someone arrived. My heart dropped aware of what this meant for some family. Maybe it was a life-saving hope, maybe it was a crisis newly made. Whatever else, your child does not come by Mediflight for a birthday party.

From the hospital, I could walk down 3rd Street or 4th Street to get Family House. If I took 3rd Street, Spark Social was on the way. To visit Spark, a food truck paradise with fire pits and S'mores, was my dream every time. Spark was not always open. Its grand opening sprang up with a flourish, a bang and free sangria. Sarah from Family House attended with me. She was my first friend in the city. It was one of those moments I sought to recapture and hold onto, like going into a bookstore.

For privacy, people in San Francisco grow clumping bamboo around industrial fences. It is beautiful in its own urban-tech way. The string lights are a celebration inviting me to eat, drink and be merry, and to feel normal again. This modern industrial meets succulent meets corroded metal architecture lines the walk to Family House which is equally sleek and modern and minimal. It was beautiful at first, but my home is filled with wood and antiques, life and history. Family House began to feel cold. I kept thinking of buying a watercolor print quilt for the rock-hard bed.

Every morning at Family House, with or without Kyle, I followed my routine. It reminded me who I am and what I am about. There was sure to be disorientation without it. The routine required I wake, exercise, dress, prepare my face and walk to Peter when the day nurse begins her shift. The routine boosts my heart.

When I returned at night to Family House, my heart fell a little each time resigned to this reality. I was alone.

In this impersonal house, I saw vestiges of my children and I recalled the ways they played here when we were together. Then it felt more like a home: a safe place apart from medical intervention. With each waking, I thought of God, exercised, and thought of coffee, a medium latte, triple shot. The cool air was a bittersweet relief from inland 102-degree heat.

A woman volunteering her time to bake and decorate cupcakes for people at Family House gave me a look like my children were deprived when I said "no, thank you" to her offer of evening sweets to my children. So, I wrote an article about food,[1] because of donated Starbucks pastries; and how I told myself I deserved that treat...every morning. Then I sold that article and earned income.

Ordinarily, I bought coffee at Peet's Cafe in the hospital. My routine gave me obligations to fill, as if I had a life, as if I was more than a medical mom.

With a Starbucks gift card, I walked across the street from Family House. My parent badge stayed tucked away in my Everlane tote until I arrived at the hospital to give the illusion I was local. When I met people, sometimes I said, "I'm here on business."

Or perhaps I said, "I'm soaking up the city like a writer."

That's not true. As much as I wanted to, I never actually lied. I actually said, "I am visiting a family member in the hospital," never saying it was my son.

For all the time that passed, a part of me was still the same person I was a year ago. The same tricks seemed to save me.

In some ways, emotionally managing Peter's condition was easier because I compared him to my other children. Having a few healthy children protected me from the self-blame and showed me Peter was learning and growing like a normal, non-medically complex child. That said, there were many challenges that come with balancing the needs of three children against the need of the one.

It took vulnerability to ask for help from my support systems at home. As something necessary and good, asking

---

[1] Kathryn Anne Casey, "Food on a Stage" *Mind & Spirit.* June 5, 2015. http://mindspirit.com/food-on-a-stage/

for help is another sacrifice to make for the sake of my family. The goal was to accept aid when offered. In a calm moment, I made a list of things people could do that I might more easily remember when we received general offers, but I never gave the list to anyone.

My support systems in the hospital included social work, child life specialists, music therapists, and so on. There was more than met the eye during our first tour. It took a while to learn what was available and see how it could benefit Peter or me.

We re-worked the spousal dynamic. It required an objective look at what each person contributed to the normal balance. I am the planner. When I was gone, and my mind was occupied with hospital business, I could not plan for my spouse or children. Kyle and others had to coordinate for themselves.

Every hospitalization, no matter if it is less worrisome than others, was a sort of crisis because our family was separated. In times of crisis, things cannot be as I would have them. My husband was not to blame if things did not function at the same caliber. An entire person was missing from the home dynamic. Learning to accept that was part of the acceptance of difficult times.

There are a handful of things I focused on in keeping the heart of our family life pumping even in my absence. After our Easter fiasco, I was determined to have a back-up San Francisco plan for every holiday. My vision for home would be simple enough to translate should Peter end up in the hospital.

This was a gift to our children. Each child's birthday was celebrated. In fact, we were able to make it such a celebration that when it came time for Peter's first birthday, I could do nothing. He was too young to understand, and so I let it go. I had reached my limit.

"Life does not stop when we get to the hospital," I tell myself. Christmas still came. Easter came. Birthdays were a big deal.

During Peter's first admission, I put off asking my parents directly to bring the children. Back then, the two-hour drive seemed like a big deal. My tank was empty when they said we would stay longer. I fell apart in tears.

After that, we kept our plan of weekend visits and communicated that plan to the children. "We do not know if Peter will still be in the hospital, but if he is, we will see each other on Saturday."

We never told them when we hoped he would be discharged until it was certain. This approach gave us things to look forward to and hope for, without getting their hopes up.

During visits we maintained our routine, limiting the time in the hospital room to keep the kids sane. We went to mass together. They went to the playroom. They knew what to expect and were excited to visit.

We persisted in communicating with our children at age-appropriate levels what was happening to Peter. "Fever," "infection," "sick," and "medicine" were household words.

"Peter has a fever...

"The doctors are working hard to find out why he has a fever...

"They'll work hard to keep him comfortable and give him medicine...

"Then he'll stay a little longer until he is strong enough to go home."

To my four-year-old, "Peter has a fever, and we are going to the hospital...but we'll see you on Saturday."

In times of uncertainty, I contacted the Child Life Specialist for advice.

Feelings were common topics in the house. Every time, I told Miriam, "I am sad to be away from you; I'll miss you and will be so happy to see you again...it is hard when we have to go."

She sensed when I was worried about Peter. When she shared her feelings with me, I listened or said, "Sometimes, I feel that way, too."

She wanted to comfort me when I cried. I let her but did not seek her out even though her hugs relieve me.

Miriam was part of the equation, even though I should like to shield her from all the pain. Though she felt what happened, we never put on her the responsibility of keeping the family together. She could engage or disengage, cry or play. However, she responded was welcome.

In order to do this for the children, I had to take care of myself. It was always difficult in times of crisis to step outside myself and talk to the kids, but I tried.

Parenting is a thousand little moments. What happened today would not define my children's future or who they are bound to be. It is okay to fall short a little each day. It is the thousand little moments added together that create the tapestry of our lives. For whatever influence the lesser moments have, there are greater moments that are equally, if not more, powerful than those.

Chapter 23

The Assumption of Mary

For the Lord himself, with a word of command, with the voice of an archangel and with the trumpet of God, will come down from heaven, and the dead in Christ will rise first. Then we who are alive, who are left, will be caught up together with them in the clouds to meet the Lord in the air. Thus we shall always be with the Lord. (1 Thessalonians 4:16-17)

The Immaculate Conception is the day the Catholic Church celebrates God's gift of redemption to Mary, through the merits of Christ's cross, applied retroactively in order to prepare a place fitting for God-made-man to dwell. In the same way, he applied the glory of his second coming retroactively by assuming her into Heaven, body and soul.

In this, he honors his mother and shows us the way.

It is one of those days of promise.

It was a great day for me. Last year, I read post after post relating the Assumption to the Theology of the Body and resurrection of the dead. None of these resonated.

Celeste was the only deceased person I ever held in my arms, the same person I held within my body. This girl leapt with joy as John the Baptist did in utero. With the glow of angels around her, she died before she had a chance to breathe the air if she would have breathed at all. We did not see her body as it was. At our request, the nurse placed her bonnet on her head before we saw her.

There were two children already waiting for me in Heaven, but I never saw them, never held them. There are other *dearly departed* in Heaven we long to be with, but we did not see them often on earth. My body was primed to detect her every movement, as it was with all my children. The year's celebration was different than before. When I think of Heaven now, it is a richer vision than ever before.

"Then we who are alive, who are left, will be caught up together with them in the clouds to meet the Lord in the air" (1 Thessalonians 4:17).

These are days of promise. I will see her perfect body, restored and complete, not as she grew, but whole.

It is easy to accept what God has on resurrection days like this. That is what these days are for: to carry us through the valley and dark times with the light of God's promise. They are moments of Transfiguration to keep in mind as we travel the Way of the Cross. Let us pause and celebrate, seeing the way it went with Mary, and how it will go with us, should we fight the good fight, and hold fast to the faith.

Chapter 24

The Coronation of Mary

After this I had a vision of a great multitude, which no one could count, from every nation, race, people, and tongue. They stood before the throne and before the Lamb, wearing white robes and holding palm branches in their hands. (Revelation 7:9)

As the priest proclaimed:

And so, with Angels and Archangels, with Thrones and Dominions, and with all the hosts and Powers of heaven, we sing the hymn of your glory, as without end we acclaim:

Holy, Holy, Holy Lord God of hosts. Heaven and earth are full of your glory. Hosanna in the highest. Blessed is he who comes in the name of the Lord. Hosanna in the highest. (Isaiah 6:3, Revelation 4:8)

In my mind's eye, I saw a vision of Celeste around the throne of God, not a baby without a brain, but a woman, made in God's image, experiencing the fullness of the beatific vision, whole and complete.

Four months passed since the day she died.

Peter sat beside me, on top of my book and cell phone, on an Art Nouveau-era walnut framed bed covered with a Miami palm print quilt. He stuffed sunglasses in underwear from the clean laundry pile left on the bed. Peter crushed a holy card and placed it in my hand. I saw him glance around, looking for a way to escape and toddle to the garage where he last saw his father leave 10 minutes ago with Peter's siblings to deliver them to the grandparents' house.

He was eager to explore. Peter could find me anywhere in the house in 60 seconds or less. His toddler cry of heartache when some piece of trash has been taken from him could stir the hardest heart, except those of his seasoned parents. We marveled at his distress, as we would at the distress of any toddler.

His cry of pain was quieter than that, more restrained, more breathless, like he was shocked it could happen. There was another cry beyond definition. He threw himself backward, and I never knew what was wrong. I just held on. If he did it for long enough, I put him to bed. After a moment, he quieted down and went to sleep.

In those days, I could not put him to bed too carelessly. With relaxed clothing and unsupervised time, he tore off the dressing that protected his Broviac site from exposure to the elements, bacteria and fungus. Another sterile dressing change came swiftly. It took three people to comfortably change that dressing. In a pinch, we could use only two sets of hands. My 6-year old daughter assisted me. Because I am particular about the stress loop in his catheter, I always serve as the primary dresser.

The boy turned pages, pointed, clapped for himself, stuck things in cups, put Mega Blocks together and was happiest in a game of peek-a-boo, especially when it involved full body movements around the house. He would master hide-and-seek if we tried it.

Life at home continued during this two-month hiatus from hospital admissions. With a 14-hour TPN cycle and no longer using the G-tube, life between 8 a.m. and 6 p.m. was normal.

The people and nurses who were part of my life were gone. The quiet of the hospital tempts me when I have forgotten how terrible it is to be separated.

House projects were completed. Decorations made. Gifts prepared. Parties thrown. With each commitment, I wondered if I would have to break it. Did I dare to commit at all? I was beginning to dare again.

The children forgot what it was to be separated and have Peter in the hospital. During the little scares that arose in these two months, they saw the suitcase, heard the possibility and the memory crept back into the minds to cast a shadow over their faces. Then they remembered. Then I remembered what it was to say goodbye, to be back on that side of the mountain.

We have no choice. After returning home following a four-hour Emergency Dept. visit, the children made the joy that much more profound. They already forgot the crisis. It is as if I went for coffee. The clothes I packed returned to their drawers and hangers as I turn the corner and put the memory behind me. The toiletry bags stayed packed because the time would come again. Let's not fool ourselves.

Adapt or die. This was my phrase for two years. Do my best to take on the challenge, stretch my mind, learn new skills, weather the emotions, or collapse into a fetal position and never get up again. The latter is not an option. As a mother, it never was.

In the conversation about miscarriage, I often said, it was easier to move through the grief because I had to keep talking to Miriam. There might be tears or dark days, but I have to keep talking to her. She needs her mother. They all do.

Life must go on.

Someone must do the dishes.

On those days I did less. I cried more. But I kept going. I kept climbing.

"The day would come when God would fill what he had emptied." Whatever trials I endured, they would not last forever. I focused on the mountaintop. At one side of the mountain, where the switchback curved around, I looked down to see the meadow with a narrow brook and sprinkles of wildflowers in the valley below. Every time I turned that corner, I cheered internally, "That's the reward! That is where we'll go when we've accomplished what we set out to do!"

Climbing the mountain was trying, requiring all the endurance one could muster. I could complain and dwell on our tears; or I could focus on the future, the goal, the reward.

On the clear, sunny days, I recalled, the rain that made these days possible. On the path, we journeyed somewhat where it was dry and difficult, but then again, the path turns, and we face the meadow. There, would I feel the gentle spring sun.

The path turns, the vistas disappear, the cloud cover renews. This is life.

On one hand, I could simply endure the days we do not like, or we could find the good they hold. It is not only the sunny days that matter. The days of promise are not the only times we feel can hope. Those days fuel the days of rest. The good that comes from them translates to a new setting and can be applied in a new way. At one time, it felt like the difficult times were all there was. "Here we go again," "when will it end?" were our slogans. As we curled up in the good times, the difficult times seemed far away, increasing the shock when they did return.

This was the lesson for me. The good times are good, but they will change, and that's okay. The rough times are rough, but they will change, so let us not lose hope. Indeed, the rain makes it so we can appreciate the light of day all the more. It clears the air, brightening the sky. Hard times force us to pause and evaluate priorities, sometimes dropping the things in life we put up with as a matter of convenience. After the work of hard times, the rest of the good times feels all the sweeter, and living it intentionally makes it more restorative than if we never struggled at all.

Christ walked this way perfectly. He is with us as we walk it today. Even as we endure, be it in good times or in bad, I keep in mind the mountaintop, our destination, our goals, the reasons we press on.

Conclusion

For two years, life felt like walking up a dusty, dry switchback trail with the sun beating down and only occasional glimpses of the meadow. I felt young and small in my isolation, bewildered at the swirl of the strange happenings around me.

Yet as my high school English teacher said to me, "This too shall pass." I did not look for the ending, I did not demand of God that our cup should be filled, but the days did pass; our cup filled to the brim once more.

Peter is alive and well, singing, dancing, and making merry with his three older siblings, and younger sister, Stella, who came into our lives quite by the Providence of God who knows best what we need. Weekly deliveries of TPN still come to our door, I still pack an ice chest with his medical supplies whenever we go for a day trip, but we go for day trips.

The Rosary concludes with the "Hail Holy Queen" supplicating the Virgin Mary to intercede for us, mourning and weeping in this valley of tears.

During a horseback ride in the Sierra Nevada, Miriam, Regina and I climbed the stone steps out of the Emigrant Wilderness in Stanislaus National Forest. We crossed a bridge over rapids, with a waterfall in view, cascading down granite boulders, dressed in pine trees. Wildflowers grow from the cracks when enough earth is settled to support a seed. The sky overhead was a deep sky blue, painted with wispy white clouds here and there.

An image of the PICU flashed through my mind as I beheld the glory of the scene, choking back an unexpected sob. Scars of a broken heart blend with the new tissue. I may

193

never experience the majesty of God or his creation without feeling simultaneously the depths of where we have been. And yet, I rarely seem to go about without the store of treasures from the journey: the walks, the flowers, the relationships with Dr. Posner, Fr. Raphael, and Summer, who each illuminated the darkness, their own stories unknown to me at the time.

At our monthly visit to San Francisco for routine appointments with people who love Peter, I feel the sun and the breeze on my face as we stop at Mariposa Park outside Benioff Children's Hospital. I smell the scent of California native plants, the sagebrush, the fuchsia, the ceanothus. This routine with all its sensory input beckons me away from the present to a time when I trusted God with all my heart. Peter calls me back to my senses to admire what he can do in the jungle gym.

I thought it would always be a dusty switchback, alone and on foot. But there will be days when we ascend the mountain within a group, led by a guide, trusting the horse, contemplating breathtaking vistas at every turn, with a loving voice to cheer and distract us when we get too frightened.

Onward we travel through paths unknown, never alone. When we dare to depend on Him as Mary did, we begin to grasp the mystery of how one could be resurrected, appearing unrecognizable, transformed through death and new life, and identifiable only by the marks of suffering. My Lord and my God! It is through this path we become more fully ourselves, more fully the creatures God meant us to be, meant for himself. And through all that darkness, we find joy.

O Clement, O Loving, O Sweet Virgin Mary,
Pray for us O Holy Mother, that we may be worthy of the promises of Christ.

Made in the USA
Monee, IL
27 July 2022